MW01278302

What's Love Got To Do With It?

Searching for life amidst the chaos of living

Steve McCoy

Earthborn LLC

For my kids

Thanks for teaching me

how to be a dad

Contents

Foreword

I'm a cynical old preacher.

I would prefer to call it "realism" but sometimes it's worse than that. I've cleaned up after more suicides, buried more babies, stood by more death beds and heard more confessions than I can even remember. Not only that, I've been conned, manipulated and lied to so much, that I've become wary of politicians, commercials and, particularly, of religious words and testimonies.

But it's not just "them"... it's me, too. Sometimes I'm so phony that I can hardly stand myself.

The upside of "cynicism/realism" about myself and others is that I've learned to identify the "real deal." It has a particular "feel" to it and, when you check it out, you're surprised to see that truth is... well truth. It has a way of getting under your skin and, to mix the metaphor, create light...

... and hope.

God has been gracious to me in showing me authenticity when I most needed it. Just when I was ready to run away, God has introduced me to someone who refuses to lie, to pretend or to play games –someone who asks the questions I ask and has made some existential discoveries about God, love and life that are so tangible and real that I can hardly stand it.

Steve McCoy is that kind of person and this is that kind of book.

If you like nice, acceptable, religious books that affirm the superficiality of "religious" systems and "religious" programs, you don't want to read this book because it will shake your world and take away the easy answers. This is a book that will disturb your peace and I would spare you that.

But if you're tired of the nonsense, the games and pretense and if you are ready to ask the questions and to see "light" without having pat answers, this book could change your life. If you want to see the "real deal" you're going to "rise up and call Steve McCoy blessed."

I *am* a cynical old preacher, but I'm not going anywhere. I'm bloodied, sometimes sinful and sometimes afraid, but I'm not leaving. As you will see as you read this book, there is no other place to go but God. That's the bad news. The good news is that God isn't anything like you've been told.

Steve McCoy is the "real deal" and the book you hold in your hands reflects that reality. Read it and be glad.

Steve Brown

Professor at Reformed Theological Seminary in Orlando, author and the host on *Key Life,* a nationally syndicated Bible teaching radio program

Introduction

The Search for Life

I am searching for life.

This book is about that search.

After a good number of years and many not so noble attempts, I have become convinced that this search for life is a universal search—a search that each of us engages in as we attempt to discover meaning and purpose, to find that which rewards us with happiness and joy, and to attain the satisfaction of our deep yearnings for love and honor. The search for life is fundamental to the human experience. It is not inhibited by cultural barriers nor is it constrained to a place or time in history.

Regardless of background, belief, or upbringing—to a person we each want to know and find happiness, satisfaction, and joy in living.

I've read about that search in the lives of mountain men who, in the early 1800s, left behind the comforts and conveniences of the modern cities and towns to venture into the unmapped wilderness and wander across prairies, mountains and deserts for countless miles. Some were running from something;

others were reaching for something more—the adventure of the hunt, the adrenaline of survival, a greater purpose, a bigger and fuller life, or simply the satisfaction of leaving their mark on history.

I witness the search in what I would call the adrenaline junkies of extreme sports. These are the athletes who challenge their abilities and gravity: some ride snowboards down stair rails or fly off mountain cliffs; others ride mountain bikes down narrow wooden paths high above the forest floor; others launch themselves off a ramp high into the air performing stunts that tempt disaster. Whatever the challenge and whatever the sport, they seem to embrace a reckless search for life. They hope to somehow find what they are looking for in the adrenaline rush of the trick, the validation from their peers, or the simple satisfaction of "going big."

Those of us who are more sedate and risk-averse are not precluded from engaging in the search for life. Some have chosen to search as they hide behind the safety of their monitor—gaming, blogging, trading, or working—depending on technology to satisfy their search. Those not as inclined to engage in pursuing life through technical challenges may find themselves in the world of characters created by Hollywood, living vicariously in front of a television screen.

There are many options from which we can choose to pursue life using places, activities, and people. Regardless of the activity or method we select, we use whatever means that seem appropriate at the time to achieve the life we dream about—the life we all long for—the life we must have.

It is not easy. The search is filled with disappointment, and for some it is brutal, as the journey buffets and batters them to the point that some give up and completely abandon the search. There are many reasons for any of us to give up: the frustration of always reaching and never being able to fully grasp what we long for, the constant cycle of effort and disappointment that simply wears us out, or the pain and disillusionment of living have simply become too great to bear. Perhaps some people simply get lost in their loneliness, convinced they can never obtain what they really want—the feeling of being truly alive, being loved, and being happy. Whatever the reason for giving up the pursuit, I suspect they have come to believe that the hurdles they face are too great, and the only choice left for them is to find some means to sedate the pain. Relief from the pain may come in the form of distraction in an activity, indulging in pleasure, or finding a convenient sedative—anything that can reduce the turmoil, at least temporarily—no matter the cost.

I have heard people say, "life happens," which is an abbreviated way of saying that life always has its trouble and heartache. All of us deal with troubles and heartaches, and we all search for relief from the disappointments. My efforts and your efforts may take different avenues, but we are not all that different from one another and the common desire to find life. We each suffer and celebrate the common issues of living.

That is not to say that we are all the same; there are, of course, many differences between us. We differ in our core beliefs and the values that have shaped us and that guide our choices and decisions. We differ in our experiences and in our individual histories. There are differences in how we look, in how we think, and in how we view the world. Our hobbies, our tastes, our jobs, our families—each of us are different in many ways.

The differences are important, and those differences are a part of what makes each of us unique. It is in front of this back drop of unique individuality that our individual searches play out. Our search is the common thread as we look to discover satisfaction in life, to live with love, happiness, and joy—to find fulfillment with the contentment of simply *being*.

No third-grader ever dreams of growing up to become a loser, a drug addict, a prostitute, or to enter into a loveless marriage. No one starts out as a destructive and hateful person. What is it that happens along the path of life that fractures the soul of a third grader, shaping her into a person she never wanted to be and a life that she never wanted to live? How is it that so many find themselves in an empty and lifeless existence? What is it that drives a person into destruction and ruin? What happened to the childhood dreams of happiness and joy? How do we come to believe that we can only find life in that which eventually destroys us and that there is no other option?

This book is about my search to discover life, my efforts to hang on to my dreams, to answer my questions, and to discover the life I imagine. You will not find quick or simple answers here. You will find some of my conclusions, but as or more important than the conclusions are the questions you find here—questions that sometimes I am afraid to ask. Yet when I find the courage and ability to put words to them, they have proven to be the most useful in my journey to discover life. The questions have helped me to know myself and this world a little better. Putting words to these questions have helped to expose my pretenses and have helped me in changing my mind. They are helping me to find my way.

It is my genuine hope that as you reflect on my journey and my questions, you might find words to your own questions and insight into your own journey. I hope that you also find encouragement to press on and continue, and not give in to despair. I do expect you to see in this effort of mine some flaws and failures in my thinking and efforts. And I hope it helps you to be honest with your own thinking and efforts. Whatever you find, I hope you don't miss the hunger and thirst of the search. They are vital in the journey to discover life.

I can only guess as to what your questions are or what prompted you to pick up this book. Perhaps in your search you have suffered through broken promises, or endured abusive relationships, or maybe loneliness seems to be your closest companion. Perhaps you are one of the very tired— exhausted from the shallow and simple solutions offered by the well-meaning. Maybe the confusion and chaos, the disappointment and sorrow of life have simply led you to believe that love is a myth, an empty promise, and it has nothing whatsoever to do with life.

I can't promise you that by reading this book you will find an end to the confusion and chaos or the disappointment and sorrow of your search. I wish I could. I can promise you that in the midst of it all—the confusion and chaos, the disappointment and sorrow—is where God most often shows up and brings life with Him. Don't despair. Ultimately, there is both light and life in this journey, and you can find it. He promised. I hope that you might find the courage to join me in discovering the passion and dreams that have been planted within our hearts and the audacity to pursue life as it was meant for us to live.

In his book, "Out of the Silent Planet" C.S. Lewis wrote, "You cannot see things till you know roughly what they are." Perhaps you will be able to see roughly a side of life that is all too easy to miss—life lived simply, honestly, and openly with courageous and contagious love: a life that is only found in Him.

In it all, I hope that you begin to understand what love has got to do with it.

Blessings

Steve

One

In Search of God Knows What

"Sometimes I feel like I'm just existing—I'm not really living. I'm only watching the time slip away." —Natalie Grant

"And I still haven't found what I'm looking for." —U2

The journey begins

Sometimes I've been told to "get a life." On a few occasions I have even given that advice to others. Frankly, there are times when I would like someone to tell me *how* I should go about "getting a life."

There are so many ups and downs, so much chaos and confusion in this journey that is called life, and frankly it is wearing me out. To say that I often feel tired and exhausted from the effort would be an understatement. I don't mean to complain. My life and this journey I've traveled have not been all that bad—at least by comparison. It just hasn't turned out the way I thought it should. I looked forward with so much anticipation to getting out of school and being able to shed the routine and demands of the schedules, studying things that seemed to hold little relevance to my life, and the dreaded hurdles called tests that allowed me to advance on only to face yet another hurdle.

After graduating from the routine of school, I found I needed to shoulder the responsibility of earning a wage to pay for—first for my car, then my apartment, and then the list just kept building—food, insurance, gas, utility bills, maintenance, and medical bills, to name a few. I traded a forty-hour work week for a paycheck and counted the days to the weekend. What I had to look forward to was a faint hope that somewhere in the future, maybe in about forty years I could possibly retire. And then what? After forty or fifty years, what's next? Is there another hurdle I must overcome in retirement, or is that all I have to look forward to?

This was not what I expected.

After finishing school and getting a job, I met a beautiful woman. We were married and began our family. I like being married to my wife, and I love my kids. But I wasn't prepared for the added responsibilities of being a husband and father and the work it demanded to build this family. I wasn't prepared for the relational confusion of being a husband or the chaos of three children and all that it added to my growing list of responsibilities. It was both rewarding and demanding all at once, but ...

It was not what I expected.

In the middle of my growing responsibilities, I think I got lost. It's not that I didn't know *where* I was or *who* I was. What I mean is that there was a growing sense somewhere within me that something was missing. But I didn't know what. Wasn't this the American Dream: a wife, kids, a house, and two cars? Didn't I have all I had ever hoped for? Was there something more that I needed to do? Was there something wrong with me? What was missing?

Maybe in all of the responsibility and busyness of life I had overlooked something, something important about how to live, something that would help me recapture the *me* that was lost, that would make me feel complete. I was thirsty and feeling as if I had been given a drink of cola to satisfy my thirst, when what I really wanted was water. I got a wet, syrupy liquid that goes down okay, but all it did was leave me thirstier and give me cavities.

I have stumbled into rare occasions along the journey that offered me a brief taste, a "wet your whistle," if you will, drink of life. They were brief, fleeting moments when for some unknown reason, everything seemed to come together with a sense of deep gratitude and satisfaction. It was the *me* I was looking for—the *me* I wanted to be—and the moments provided me with a brief glimpse of the kind of life I wanted to live. But those moments were just that: *moments*.

Those moments didn't last as long as I would have liked them to, and no matter how hard I tried I could find no way to recapture them. They left me wanting more. As satisfying as it was to experience those moments, the memories of them became a mere tease to me, as I tried and hoped to recreate them. As refreshing as they were, they also increased the awareness of my thirst.

I am not one given to making things more complicated than they already are. As I have already mentioned, my choices made life more complicated as I lived out my journey. Am I supposed to chill out or try harder, live intentionally, or let it happen? All of my efforts to find my way back to those moments, all of the effort to "do the right thing" or "let it be" or "go with the flow" have done little to recapture even a moment, let alone to help me find life as I want to live it.

My efforts have often only stirred things up. Much like stirring the creek bottom when you are bending down to get a drink, it only disturbs the mud and dirties the water. Frankly, my life has enough mud in it already, enough complications on its own without stirring things up and making it worse. My efforts sometimes seem to work against me, but what am I supposed to do?

I'm still thirsty.

The hurdles I faced, the milestones I achieved, all held out a carrot that life would get better—once I accomplished the next goal. Once I achieved the objective—when I made it to sixth grade, once I got my driver's license, after I graduated from high school, found a job, when I met my soul mate and began a family—all of these milestones held the promise and expectation that life would be much better. I'm not sure why I thought it would be better. I suppose I thought life would be better because of my achievements, because I had reached the goal, because I had obtained the carrot.

But it didn't turn out that way. It didn't turn out the way I expected.

I expected more from my achievements. I expected that life would somehow get easier and then, because of the satisfaction of my achievements, I would be able to greet each morning with more energy; I would be able to face each new day with expectation and appreciation. I thought that I would be able to live more in those moments that I described, and I didn't expect to have to work so hard to overcome the endless mundane moments that filled most of my days. I didn't expect the nagging insecurity that left me wondering about my place and purpose in the order of life.

My expectations were high but not with a blind eye towards my faults and character flaws. I was not trying to ignore reality and I was keenly aware that I had my short comings and failures. I hoped to learn to live a life where I met my short comings with honesty, acknowledging my failures quickly without melting beneath them in shame and humiliation. Is that too unrealistic? Isn't that worth reaching for? Wouldn't it be wonderful to live life with gratitude and expectation each day or even most days instead of stumbling under the weight of the chaos of living, confused about what to do next?

Surely it is possible to find more of the life I want. When I look around, it appears that other people are able to enjoy this kind of life. Just look at the heroes that we see in the news and on TV. They have the "big life," right? They have adoration, fame, and fortune. They win the game at the buzzer; they get the big trophy and the parade after the game. To be honest, I'm envious. I'd like to be the hero. I'd like the adoration. And I'm envious of their fame and fortune. I'm envious of their skills and talents. I don't need to save the world, but if only I could win once or capture a little recognition for myself. Then perhaps I could experience the same kind of life they have—the life I long for.

I have no expectations that I will ever achieve hero status. I don't have the abilities or the opportunities of those heroes we watch on TV. But do you think it is still possible for me to find a way to be satisfied with and enjoy *me*, with the abilities *I've* been given, and the people *I* am able to touch and take pleasure in? Is it possible that I could be happy with the satisfaction of making my small contributions to the world? Could I find the life I want in living a simple, unpretentious life?

If it is not possible for me to find a way to enjoy the me that I am and the obscure life that I might live, then is there any hope for me to find the life that I long to live? This search is sometimes very challenging, and often complicated. It seems that the harder I try, the more difficult it becomes, and I find life impossible to get right. I just don't understand. The things I thought I once understood, I'm not so sure of anymore.

Sing from the soul

I have a fourteen-month-old granddaughter. She has all of life ahead of her—her dreams and aspirations are not yet formed in her thoughts. She has little care in her world, except perhaps how to get what she wants in the moment. For the past three months or so, each time she visits us she goes to work pulling herself up and attempting to navigate around on her own shaky legs. Sometimes she uses the furniture, the wall, or the glass front on the gas fireplace to help her get up.

Her dad doesn't want her to touch the glass fireplace, fearing that someday it will be hot. For now it isn't. It is never on.

My granddaughter doesn't understand what the word *hot* means. It doesn't matter how hard we try to explain it to her, she simply doesn't understand what the word means. She can say *hot* and she knows she is not supposed to touch the glass, but she doesn't understand *hot*, and she won't ...

...until she feels it.

Then she'll know.

I confess. I watch American Idol. I like hearing the young singers. Each year there are one or two standouts, and each year they are told by the judges to sing with conviction. They want them to make the songs their own.

Then I heard one of the contestants say that she was going to sing from her soul, and it dawned on me that what the judges want is for a singer to do more than simply sing. They want the singer to be willing and able to emotionally climb into the song, to enter into it, and own it. The best singers are able to sing as if the joy belongs to them, as if the tears are their own, as if the pain is from their own broken heart, and the laughter is from their own funny bone.

That is what it means to own the song.

If you want to sing it and own it, you have to be willing to feel it.

Many of the contestants on the show are good singers. Some sing exceptionally well. They can sing upbeat songs as if they were happy, and sad songs as if they were sad. But they don't own the joy and pain they sing about.

They don't feel it.

They are only pretending.

My granddaughter will learn about *hot* when she feels it. It will hurt, and then she will know. Some of the best musicians birth their music from the disappointments and failures of their life experiences. If I am to enter into the song of my life, to be able to live life from my soul, then I must sing my song, the song of my life without pretense. I must allow myself to feel the pain, the joy, the tears, and the delight.

Life is quickly filled with responsibilities–responsibilities that we can get lost in. I became lost in the responsibilities to my wife, my children, my church, and my employer. I had a good job. I was a productive member of society and my church. I learned as a young boy how to behave well, or at least which rules were important and I applied my good behavior to my responsibilities.

I served.

I gave.

I played well with others.

I believed that fulfilling my obligations and duties would be enough to satisfy my thirst for life.

It wasn't.

It left me frustrated, and there were many times that I would have turned off my thirst if I could have. The problem is that there is no "on" or "off" switch for this thirst and it is impossible to simply ignore it.

I didn't comprehend that like my granddaughter, I needed to *feel* it to understand it, and that turning it off is no answer.

Rene' Descartes was the one who said, "I think, therefore I am." To which I say, "I am what?" I like to think, but simply thinking isn't all that satisfying for me, and it just isn't enough. Knowing I exist does not satisfy my thirst for life. I have found *existence* in the five-day grind of work, fulfilling my responsibilities while waiting for the weekend reprieve. I have found *existence* in the lonely weekends when I was unable to find something to fill the emptiness and nothing to live for that was bigger than me.

Existing is simply being thirsty or trying not to be thirsty. Existing may prove life, but there is more to living than simply existing.

What is life supposed to be all about anyway? Is there something that will quench my thirst and help me to find what I'm looking for?

Life is a common and casual word. I mean, we use it or hear it nearly every day. We all know that we have life. It's not all that complicated is it? We are born. We grow. We breathe.

All the while, our heart muscles pump blood through our veins. All of this happens without conscious effort.

It is life.

And because we think, our self-awareness validates and confirms that we are alive. This is all good, and it may be enough for some, but ...

I'm still thirsty.

Is finding happiness only a fairy tale?

Am I alone in my discontent and dissatisfaction?

Must I simply endure my thirst for life, or is there an answer—a fountain that will quench this thirst?

False hopes: the great con and the universal search for happiness

I am surrounded by images and promises of the life I want. They only serve to taunt me. Images of great success, fame, and fortune appear daily on commercials and in magazines. Each sport lifts up the best of the game; Michael Jordan, Tiger Woods, and Dale Earnhardt, Jr. to name a few. The music industry displays their greats (who are too numerous to mention) appearing in videos and on CD covers. The business world covets their own elite executives such as Warren Buffet and Bill Gates. Each of these people portrays an image of success, having excelled in their given field, applying their talents and ideas to an art or craft. We read their books, buy their posters, and hold them up as examples.

They are envied. They have it all, and in unison the culture bows before them in adoration, because they look as if they live life big and full; they apparently have all of the benefits and glory of living.

I confess. I wish that I could live as big as they are able to. It certainly seems that they are enjoying life as it was meant to be lived. From all appearances, they seem to have found it— recognition, wealth, and success. They don't seem to wrestle with life as I do. They don't appear to be thirsty.

And I want what they have.

And, then I discover that the happy Hollywood couple has announced a separation, and a messy divorce follows. Or the executive is found to be "human" and the less attractive aspects of his or her life are exposed to public view and humiliation. And it has become common news to hear of athletes using performance enhancement substances to give them the competitive edge, helping them gain and maintain their positions of greatness.

Upon closer look, maybe they are not finding the satisfaction I thought they had. Maybe they aren't living as big and well as I thought they were? If that is true, then where is the incentive for me to pay the price to live the "big life" they are living if after all of my effort, it only leaves me once again— thirsty?

It is too high of a price to pay if there is no satisfaction for my thirst. Is that really success? Is that the better life?

Then, as if an answer to my prayers, the television ads promise me in my ordinary, average-guy life that I can find everything I could possibly want to obtain a blissful life. My hope grows as I think that at last I will be able to come to the end of this restless search. For three simple payments of $29.99 I can have the product I always wanted and find the satisfaction, the fulfillment of what I long for. Then my relationship troubles will be over. I can have clean teeth, a brighter smile, and more friends—all because of my new irresistible self. Or, if I buy the new convertible and drive to the mountains with the top down and my hair blowing in the breeze, maybe that will do the trick? Or, I could make a discrete purchase of a male enhancement product, and it will provide lasting satisfaction—blissful happiness and the life I've always wanted!

At least that's what they say.

They wouldn't lie to me would they?

I see the images. Even when I know the claims are bogus, it still leaves me thirsty. I wish it were true that I could transform my life by purchasing a certain product. I feel so inadequate, so exposed, so incapable of living life as I imagine it should be. I admit that sometimes I have recklessly thrown myself upon the promises, falling for the bait, hoping that this time, maybe it will come true. Maybe this time I'll find what I'm looking for in that special purchase.

I want life. I am so tired of the absurd promises and the fake heroes. I've tried more promises and attempted to imitate more pretentious people than I care to admit. Sometimes I simply don't have the energy. Sometimes I just watch as others try, wondering if it will work for them, wondering if they'll find life.

Some seem to.

Most have not.

Over time, and with many failed attempts to resolve my dilemma, I've found it easier to simply give in to cynicism, as my futile attempts have failed to satisfy the emptiness I feel. I have fallen far short of greatness. I have no fame and am far less significant than those promoted in the media as being successful. I have little hope of ever being on the top of anyone's list—so much for fame and fortune.

Once again, I wonder if it might be possible to lose my desire for life, because it seems that there is nothing that can really satisfy it.

And then I stumble upon a part of the Bible where Jesus says that this unquenchable thirst of mine is a good thing. He seems to be saying that this lingering thirst I have will lead me to find life. It is as if He *wants* me to be hungry and driven. He promises that I'll find satisfaction in this search for life. In fact, He said that He came to bring life—plentiful, copious, bountiful, overflowing life.

If I don't give up ...

If I keep looking ...

He said my thirst would be quenched, and that I'd be filled. [1]

I find some encouragement in that affirmation of my search.
Yet, telling a thirsty man that feeling thirsty is a good thing
hardly satisfies the desire for a long fresh drink of water. I
really want life in "good measure, pressed down, shaken
together and running over." [2]

Whatever that means.

Maybe He can help me understand how to climb into life and
sing it from my soul?

Life as You promised

I like promises, and the promises that Jesus makes are not to
be taken lightly. But I'm confused at how being thirsty is
satisfying. Perhaps I'm just slow. What I do know is that I'm
still thirsty.

Let me interrupt myself for a moment, lest you think that my
thirst is based in simple boredom, or that I'm complaining
over not getting what I wanted, or that I'm jealous of those
who have more. My life, at least from outward appearances—
the things I can say and brag about—has turned out pretty
well. Some aspects of my life have turned out much better
than I thought they might and far better than I deserve. For
example, as I said earlier, I'm married to a beautiful woman. I
have three children teaching me how to be a father. Early on,
we were able to purchase a home for our growing family. I've
worked for one of the companies viewed as the best in the US
and I've been healthy enough to play hard when the
opportunity presented itself.

No, my journey has not been boring, without accomplishment, or occasional successes. It has been busy and rewarding in the sense of reaching and accomplishing and learning. I simply have a nagging sense that there is more to the journey than what I have already learned and more than what I have already accomplished. This sense that there is more to life than what I've learned and accomplished stems from the unsatisfied thirst within me. It all may sound to you like complaining; if it does, it is my inability to say it any better. It's not that I am bored, and I don't mean to complain. It is just that in all of the busyness, I still have this nagging thirst. Something in my life is missing, and I am trying to discover what it is.

I live with the normal tension and difficulties of life, the common chaos and confusion that people experience in reaching for dreams and trying to make life better. I am not exempt from disappointment, shattered dreams and failure. I've had my share of each.

Wouldn't Jesus' promise be for me too, in the reality of the chaos and confusion of my life? I really want that—a promise of life that meets me where I live.

I want a life full with the satisfaction of accomplishment, rich with family and friends, deep with purpose and meaningful pursuits.

That is what I imagined God promised me.

Yet in all of my effort to achieve this life that I imagine, I have found myself feeling more and more trapped, confined, and restricted. At one point it honestly felt to me as if I were being smothered. I'm not trying to be overly dramatic here; this is actually the sensation I felt—as if some ever-shrinking plastic-wrap tent had been placed over me, smothering me, and forcing me to my knees.

It was in this smothering state of life that one day I opened my Bible to the promise Jesus had made, and looking toward heaven, I said, "God, you promised me life. I didn't write the promise. You did. I want it. Life as you promised. What I am living feels more like dying to me. I want life."

That was a turning point for me in my journey, the journey to see whether there was anything that could quench this thirst and offer me a way out of the suffocating plastic-wrap tent.

There are many songs written about life, hundreds of books, and thousands of people singing and talking about and around it. That's the easy part.

I want to see what life looks like! I want to live it! I want to feel it!

I want a life filled with purpose, with satisfaction, and deep, rewarding relationships. I want a life filled with wisdom to guide me through the chaos and confusion that I face every day. I want a life that I can climb into and sing as my own, that I feel, and live out loud, a *real life* possessing the elasticity to hysterically enjoy the silly tickles of the soul and strong enough to sustain me as I deal with all of my failure and all of the pain—even as I watch my father on his death bed, dying of brain cancer.

I want a life like that.

Two

Suffocating Goodness

I'm so tired of
Of all these easy solutions
I can't stand it
They're nothing but denial
I think I need a personal revolution
How can I expect the heart to sing
When I don't let the soul ever feel anything
*   -Charlie Peacock*

The problem with desire

A friend of mine recently told me that the problem with life is desire. If we could simply eliminate desire, we wouldn't have all of the troubles we have. The problems would go away. I think he was trying to say that if people didn't want what they didn't have, that if we could take away the wanting, there would be no motivation to do whatever it took for us to get the "it" we want.

Whatever the "it" might be.

In other words, without desire we would have no reason or motive to want what other people have. If we didn't want what they have, there would be no reason or motive for people to hurt other people. We simply would not want to.

If no one wanted my television, I wouldn't have to lock my doors to protect it. And no one would cut me off on the freeway, because they wouldn't want to be in front of me. There would be no drugs, because we would have no desire to escape from reality; no shady salesmen, because they would not want our money; no identity theft, because nobody would want what they don't have; no murder, no war, no rape, no bad stuff.

My friend was saying that without desire, people would simply quit doing bad stuff to each other. They would have no desire or motivation to inspire them to take negative actions.

But I don't think my friend was talking only about other people's desire. I think my friend was saying that life would be better, there would be less pressure and confusion if he could eliminate his own desire. If he didn't have the want for the *things* he thought he needed, he wouldn't feel the tension of that desire urging him to try to get those *things* to satisfy his desire. There was so much that he wanted and simply couldn't have.

If he could eliminate his desire then he wouldn't have the aspiration to be famous and important. Without desire he would have no envy of the attention and affirmation of the celebrities that seem to have it all, all the money to do what they want, when they want. Without desire he would not have to suffer the daily disappointment of waking up and knowing that he could not get what he really wanted and repeatedly feeling the distress of knowing what he wanted was hopelessly out of reach.

He didn't say it with the same words as I am using, but I wonder if my friend was simply saying that he was thirsty and looking for life too. Maybe he was simply tiring of all the effort, and his conclusion was that because there seemed to be nothing he could find to satisfy his thirst, he should try to eliminate it, rather than continue the frustrating effort. The best way to eliminate the thirst would be to eliminate the desire, the want for the thing he couldn't get. Then he wouldn't feel thirsty, and he wouldn't care.

I think what he was saying is that without desire he believed his life would be easier.

I thought about that conversation for several days. I wondered about desire and what life would be like without it. I cannot give up on desire, and even though I did not agree with him, I had to admit to myself that I had tried to eliminate my own desire as well. Unwittingly I had adopted the method as a means to manage my own life and passions. It was my attempt to control my "dark side," if you will, so that I could achieve "good" and find life.

I had used much the same logic. If I could eliminate the desire that fueled my "bad" behavior, if I could stop wanting to do the things that end up hurting me or others, if I could stop doing the things that only leave me with disappointment and guilt, then maybe I could find the life I really wanted.

I did not consciously reason my way to this conclusion. I did not sit down and think to myself that I will eliminate desire to live better. It just kind of happened. And I doubt that I would have known it unless my friend had expressed his heart to me.

Thinking back, I suppose it was due in part to my obsessed effort to live a good life and to do things the right way that led me to this suppression of desire. The logic seems sound enough; do the things that are right and good, and don't do the things that are bad and evil.

At least that is how I reasoned it out.

It seems simple enough, cull out my bad desire and leave only the desire to do good. What I didn't expect was finding that it was impossible for me to separate my bad desire from my good desire. I found both the desire to do bad and the desire to do good originated from the same source; desire.

I find the same results when I try to eliminate the pain in my life; unwittingly I eliminate feeling as I try to eliminate pain, and then I am left with no feeling. To the degree that I can't feel pain, neither can I feel enjoyment. Suffocating feeling does away with both pain and pleasure. I am left without feeling, numb to emotions. Unintentionally, I suffocated my desire to do good in my attempt to suffocate my desire to do bad, leaving me with nothing good or bad.

Frankly, it is a safer life, attempting to live with no desire. I can do most of the things I should do, fulfilling my responsibilities and never risking the failure of what I might hope or dream my life could be. I may have to sacrifice that part of my life, the heart where desire and feeling reside, to protect myself, but it is "safe."

Living this way I will never find the life I really want, but I will be able to live a *safe* life.

There are some penalties to playing it safe. To maintain this safe life, it requires that I pretend. I must pretend that I am not thirsty and that life is good. I must pretend and deny the deeper problems that I cannot control, hoping that if I ignore them, they will go away. The problem with that method of living is that if God has made me with desire and placed these desires within my heart, then I will never be free from them no matter how hard I try to eradicate the desire within me.

How am I?

I'm just fine. Thank you. Maybe today I'm even great!

And so I hide my failures. I hide my issues and my struggles. I smile when I need to and pretend to be happy. I pretend that I am not all that thirsty. But I find in all of my pretense, in all of my effort to kill my desire, I must try hardest to convince myself that I am happy and fulfilled.

As hard as I have tried to manage my desire, I find it is simply unmanageable. It will not be ignored or denied. If I attempt to push my desire down and to smother it in one area of life, it is much like a balloon and just bulges out in another area of my life. I have not been able to pacify it, medicate it, sedate it, or fulfill it.

It may be safe, but all of my efforts to pacify desire have only left me unsatisfied and unfulfilled.

Anticipation and disappointment

My brother and I found ourselves driving home from our annual hunting trip in the Cascade Mountains. Our love for the woods and mountains and our passion for hunting is our inheritance from a dad who loved the woods and taught us how to hunt, fish, camp, walk logs, and build fires. We spent many summer weekends on family camping trips or backpacking into the Cascade Mountain lakes, ever watchful for the deer or elk we might see on the way. We grew to love the outdoors because of our dad's love of the same. Both of my brothers became avid hunters, and each November we trek into the woods with our tents and gear for our annual hunting trip, much the same as dad used to do.

We may love the woods, but that does not make all of our hunting trips glorious. This particular hunt was more than a little disappointing, especially for my brother. As we made the three-hour drive home, I asked him what he enjoyed most about the hunt. His answer intrigued me.

"The planning."

That was his answer to what is the most enjoyable part of the hunting trip. That isn't the way it is supposed to be. The enjoyment should be in the experience, in the doing. The reason his answer intrigued me is that all of the anticipation and expectation is in the planning, and in the planning there is none of the risk. It is in the planning where all of the hopes and dreams live, and none of the disappointment, as the preparation and anticipation of the journey is the focus.

I thought about his comment and the many times that I had tried to make a plan for my family or one for myself. From vacations, a dinner out, or a simple afternoon of activity, there had been many attempts, and in spite of my best efforts, most times they fell far short of my expectations. Maybe it would be better to simply let things happen and not plan at all? At least then I wouldn't have to suffer the disappointment when the events did not meet the expectations of my plans.

A coworker recently took his family to Disney World. He said they had a great time. I was envious. It was an expensive trip, but perhaps that is what the Disney theme parks are all about. All you have to do is get there, and they manage the entertainment and provide an experience for you. At least the failure is not my fault when someone else is responsible for the entertainment.

If I can find someone else to blame, a scapegoat for my disappointment or failure, then there is no risk of failing. It's not my fault, and there is little to fear.

Maybe that is my problem, that I am afraid. I am afraid of where my desire might lead me if I give it some expression. I am afraid of what others will think. What if I look stupid or what if I can't succeed or what if I fail miserably?

I am afraid of dreams that can never come true, and I am distrustful of the desire within me that urges me to reach toward those dreams.

I am unable to manage this desire that I find within me. It is beyond my ability. I cannot control it. When I follow it, I often find it has left me with disappointment and failure. I reach for fulfillment, satisfaction, the glory of achievement, and greatness, but most often I am left embarrassed, guilty, and, depending on how public my intentions were, sometimes humiliated.

What do I do with this desire that does not yield itself to my efforts to restrain it? How do I let it breathe and keep it pure, not allowing a bent desire to lead me to destruction? I want to *do* good and *be* good, but I am simply not strong enough. Pretending I am good is simply masking the truth and letting the dark side of my desire run loose. I want to find life, yet even my desire for life leads me into doing things that I know I shouldn't do.

I am so tired of pretending and so tired of failing. If this desire within me is really God-given, then what am I supposed to do with it?

I must try harder to be good.

My vow
As I began my journey of faith, I read and studied my Bible. I didn't resent it. In fact, I really enjoyed it. They said it would help. It held answers to my questions and offered the secrets to finding the life I desperately wanted. So I read every

morning and most nights. Sometimes during the week I read at lunch time too. There was so much to learn and so much to discover. It was all so new and fresh to me. At times the words seemed to jump at me from the pages I was reading.

My wife and I attended seminars and Bible studies as often as we could. Soon we were asked to teach others what we had learned. We were learning new things about life, wanting to learn more and to share what we were learning. We both tried very hard to "get it right."

Along the way, I learned that I should pray every day. I also read about the very serious and committed who devoted themselves to praying for one or two hours a day. This sounded like a good idea. I was serious, and maybe this commitment would help me rise above the mundane and help me find the answers to my search for life. So I began to get up early each day and set aside time to read and pray. I thought I would start with smaller amounts of time and work up to being really serious so I decided to begin with thirty minutes of prayer.

It was early for me. I tried to read. I tried to pray, but closing my eyes, sitting in my chair looking at the ink on the page only served to lull me back to sleep after a few minutes. Kneeling didn't help either. I would fall asleep on my knees.

I felt guilty.

I needed to do better.

At one of the seminars my wife and I attended, a solution was offered. It was suggested that we make a solemn vow. It would help us move toward life. The speaker emphasized how important a vow was, especially when one makes a vow to God. It was to be a serious oath, a promise that should be kept at all costs.

So I made a vow to pray each day for five minutes. Five minutes a day.

I can do that!

I will do it!

It's only five minutes!

Before three months were up, I had broken my vow.

I had broken my promise to One who should not be taken lightly. I had failed again. I was guilty again. There was only one thing for me to do.

I made another vow.

Now this may seem stupid to you, but this time I promised never to make a vow again, because I had learned that I am not faithful enough to keep my vows. It was an important lesson in honesty, an important lesson of the truth about myself.

No more promises. No more working at trying so hard to be good, trying to get it right. I simply couldn't be good enough.

In fact I turned my eyes upward to look God in the eye, and not only did I tell Him that I would make no more vows, I told Him that I would not read my Bible or pray any more out of a sense of duty or obligation.

I would read and pray because I wanted to, out of desire, or I would not do it at all.

I was tired of feeling the suffocation of my efforts. I wanted out of the plastic tent. It was smothering me.

You may think me to be rather flakey and weak in my effort, or think that I had given up too easily.

You may be right.

Yet something had begun to stir within me. I no longer felt suffocated. I no longer felt smothered by the plastic-wrap tent. It seemed to be gone. It was as if my heart that had been gasping for air had begun to breathe freely for the first time in a long time. Perhaps it was the fresh air in the honest admission that I simply was not all that good. Maybe God was leading me, or maybe it was simply indigestion. I can't be absolutely sure. What I do know is that, for the first time in a long time there was a sense of freedom as I began to be honest with myself and attempt to follow Jesus without pretense.

To be honest with you, just because I felt free didn't mean that I was. If I jumped off a bridge, I would feel free from gravity as I rapidly approached the end of my jump. There would be little benefit or life in the ending, but the fall would give me the illusion of freedom from gravity. There are restraints in life that are there for our good and our benefit. They are not meant to destroy us, but climbing over them only leads to destruction, not freedom. The thought had occurred to me that I might be jumping over the restraints meant for my own good. Not all desire deserves to be followed or pursued, and one should always consider how tall the bridge is and what is under it before one jumps.

Also this was not an act of anger towards God as Cain did when he found that his goodness was not good enough to be acceptable to God. *What I was finding was the freedom to desire what I wanted most.*

I was finding the freedom to let my yes be yes and my no be no and to live simply and honestly before God and man.

I was discovering the freedom to feel and live.

The conflict within
I watch TV. Sometimes I watch a lot of TV. I may even be addicted to TV. I enjoy the stories that are told in the movies and in some of the programs. I am an avid channel surfer, proving my agility and masculinity. I am able to watch two or three programs at once, timing the channel changes to capture the action scenes, following the plots in each program. I never tire of seeing the good guy win or the underdog come out on top against impossible odds. I can't tell you how many times I've watched Die Hard, Lethal Weapon, or one of Sean Connery's movies.

I love a good story.

A friend recommended to me the movie *Equilibrium*. Not a particularly great movie in my opinion, but fascinating, as the story is all about controlling evil by subduing emotion and feeling through mandatory drugs and forbidding all color and any object that might evoke desire or feelings. In the plot of this story, feeling became a capital offense.

As I watched with increasing interest I was beginning to identify with the character's efforts to subdue desire as a method to control life. And even in the movie, contrary to all of the efforts used in the attempt to restrain desire and curb evil, it only served to increase the heart's susceptibility to the very emotion they were seeking to control.

One scene in particular captured my attention. A woman "offender" was being interrogated for her "feeling offense." In this scene she turned the tables on her interrogator, putting *him* on the defense, when she looked him square in the eye and asked him, "Why are you alive?" His eyes couldn't bear her gaze as he attempted to find an answer.

"I'm alive ...." He stumbled with his words, searching himself to find a valid answer to her question. "I live to safeguard the continuity of this great society." He regurgitated the propaganda of the system because he could find no other words. It was the best he could do.

"It's circular." She answered. "You exist to continue your existence. What's the point?"

The interrogator acted like a cockroach in a room that just had the light turned on. He was desperately trying to hide, so he turned the question on her.

"What is the point of your existence?"

I had become part of this conversation. I was captivated by the events and had vicariously become the interrogator, hiding from the question, turning my head from her gaze yet eager to hear her response. When I heard her response, I had to rewind the movie and listen to it again.

"To feel ... Because if you've never done it you can never know it, but it's as vital as breath, and without it, without love, without anger, without sorrow, breath is just a clock ticking."

The answer was more than I expected from a movie. I sat in my chair stunned. I rewound the scene and played it again. This movie was stirring me more deeply than I can explain. It was a message to me in surround sound and full color; I believe God was speaking to me through this movie, inviting me back to feel, to His gift of desire, to live and to life. He was giving me permission to find the passion of life, and letting me know that desire was a part of life, as He meant it to be.

This may all sound more than a little goofy to you. It's a movie, for goodness sake! It's not church or the Bible. Yet here was a place that God was speaking to me.

I'm sure He speaks to you in ways that you can understand, although, you, probably like me, doubt it when you hear Him. This was a clear message to me in a way that I could understand and in a place that I was not expecting Him to show up. Why He even bothers to bend down so low as to enter into my world and use language and illustrations of truths that I can at least partially comprehend is beyond my understanding. We simply would never be able to hear Him if He didn't speak to us in simple ways such as in a movie, so that we could understand Him better. He doesn't often let us know what He's doing; He just surprises us and shows up.

I understood.

Several months later, in a food booth at the fairgrounds, He used another friend to confirm the progress in my personal journey. After briefly catching up on what had been happening in each other's lives, my friend stated simply, "You're beginning to feel again."

It seemed to be a fluke statement in a brief and casual conversation that stuck in my mind. When I replayed it in my head, it was spoken by a still small voice, much deeper than my friends. The voice was speaking to the part of my life that had been gasping for air. It was a gentle and comforting voice, speaking to a place in my heart where life was beginning to stir, both affirming and leading me on the path that I was beginning to see more clearly.

I have spent many years obsessed with efforts of being good and attempting to avoid evil by subduing my desire. My reward for all of this effort was an ever-increasing amount of internal conflict. At first, as the conflict increased, I concluded that I must try harder to subdue both my desire and feelings. It was not immediately apparent to me that I was getting worse and not better.

I was holding on to my own goodness with all my might. It seemed to be the only means to battle my guilt and corruption, and the penalty was the death of my desire and feeling. I did not realize that all the while my own efforts were suffocating me.

Three

Wish Upon a Star

A dream is a wish your heart makes
When you're fast asleep
In dreams you lose your heartaches
Whatever you wish for, you keep

Have faith in your dreams and someday
Your rainbow will come smiling thru
No matter how your heart is grieving
If you keep on believing
the dream that you wish will come true
So dream...   [Written by: Mack David, Al Hoffman and
Jerry Livingston, used in Cinderella]

A dream is a wish your heart makes
We were in a parking lot at a hotel in Cannon Beach, Oregon
unpacking our saddle bags, when I looked up and noticed a
lady who looked to be in her early seventies walking on the
other side of the parking lot. When she noticed us, she slowed
to a pause, standing and watching at a distance with subdued
interest.

It is not unusual that someone will look, gawk or gaze in our direction when we are on a trip with our Harleys. Some will wave as we ride by, and a few will drive alongside of us as we ride on the freeway, giving us a wave and sometimes rolling down their windows to listen to the engines as we rumble down the highway. Occasionally when we park the bikes a few will venture into our circle of friends to talk about the bikes, some telling us about their dreams of owning one or what they ride, others stop by simply to admire the chrome.

One lady gave me a "thumbs up" from the front seat of her diesel pick-up truck as she left the gas station and noticed my wife and I on our bike, fueling up. Another lady with her disabled daughter in her arms, approached us in a parking lot so that her daughter could see the motorcycles and hear them when we started the engines. She said her daughter loved motorcycles.

So it was not unusual that someone would pause to look at the bikes as we ended the day's ride. It was evident that this aging woman was genuinely interested, yet reluctant to venture any closer to the commotion between the six of us as we detached saddle bags, removed travel packs, and locked down the bikes for the night.

I looked her in the eye and greeted her with, "How's it going?" I aimed my greeting as a welcome to further engage her interest and inviting her over to take a closer look.

Hesitantly she stepped into the circle as my wife and friends began to take notice of her. Greetings were exchanged as we continued preparing the bikes for the evening. Then she began to tell us that she had been a rider once, and that she had owned her own Harley until a few years ago when her family had made her sell it. No one else in her family had ridden motorcycles, she explained, and no one else in her family understood.

Her story had captured our attention, and we now were the ones pausing, wondering if we should venture any closer as we listened to her share her story and expose a part of her heart to us.

For that brief moment we shared our dreams with a woman in the autumn of her life. A casual moment that was part of a planned ride down the coast, a time for six friends to relax and enjoy each other's company as we reached for dreams of our own. Little did we know that in reaching for our dreams, we unintentionally invited an aging woman to relive and remember her passing dreams. Listening to the story and looking in her eyes, you could almost see the memories of her hair blowing in the wind as she throttled down the highway, dressed in leathers, lost in the moment.

She knew that we understood. And as she spoke of the memories, her motorcycle, and how much she loved to ride, tears began to roll down her cheeks from both the joy and pain of her memories and lost dreams. When the pain overcame the joy and the memories became more than the woman wanted to bear, she quietly returned to the task that had brought her into the parking lot in the first place.

She had exposed her heart to us. In sharing the memory of the rides she had been on, the tears that ran down her cheeks, and her hesitancy to hear about our day's ride, she had shared with us a part of her heart.

Dreams are birthed in the heart. Dreams are a fundamental part of who we are; they are the fuel of passion, and they are inseparable from the desires of life. Without dreams I am simply putting time in, spending my life without living it.

I am only a "clock ticking."

Giving a voice to my dreams opens a window into my heart, and the God-given desires that live within me.

Without dreams, how can I ever hope to find the life for which I am looking?

The danger of the heart
My daughter Andrea loves to dance.

I confess. It's my fault.

I held her in my arms as a child, listening to my favorite music as we danced around the house.

She laughed. I laughed.

These were moments of childhood cherished by both father and daughter, filled with spontaneous fun and laughter, and she usually asked for more long after I wanted to finish.

Everyone knows that Christians don't dance. But my daughter never lost her enjoyment of dancing. Even as a teenager and young adult she still loves to dance. She is no longer a child under my guidance and protection. I cannot dictate to her what she can and cannot do. And now I face a dilemma. What am I to do? Do I restrict her and withhold my approval and love until she conforms to my standards?

There are good reasons Christians don't dance. After all, dancing poses some risky and possibly compromising situations in which a young adult such as my daughter could find herself in. If I allow her to continue this pursuit, it is only a matter of time until she will inevitably find herself in these compromising situations.

What kind of people go to these dances? There simply are no "Christian" dances for her to go to.

What am I to do?

If I disallow it even from the best of motives, I would be asking her to sedate her passion for dance and smother her heart. If I press the issue it would force her to make a choice between me and dancing, a choice in which we both lose; I lose a daughter and she loses her father.

What is my responsibility to her as her father?

If life is found in the heart and the heart is found in the pursuit of dreams and desires, how do I encourage my daughter in her journey of life to enjoy the person that God has made her to be? If dancing is a God-given desire in her heart, placed there from birth, then I will never be able to tame it. In fact, my effort to do so would be fighting a battle against God's design, not to mention that it would be impossible for me to tame.

As a child she had dreams of becoming a ballerina, and with all of the practical logic I could present to her, I worked very hard to dissuade her from those dreams. It wasn't that I didn't want her to dance (Ballet is much more acceptable in Christian circles than Salsa dancing!) I simply wanted to help her see the incredible odds against her achieving a level of talent that would support her, pay for her car, her house, and the life she wanted to live.

It may have influenced her choice of professions but it didn't sedate her desire to dance. She still loves dancing. I know, it wasn't very supportive of me to attempt to dissuade her from her dreams, but frankly, I'm glad she didn't pursue it as a career.

She is not a rebellious or obstinate child. She, like her siblings, found desires and dreams that I believed would lead them astray or even hurt them. As their father, isn't it my responsibility to guide and protect them, to help them avoid those things and situations that would cause them personal damage? I have taken seriously the responsibility to nurture and protect my children. It is not an easy task, and I expect my attempts to manage their lives and guide them to safety were frequently beyond what was required of me and bordered on damage from over protection.

I find myself conflicted in my desire to protect my children and my desire for them to discover and live life for themselves. How can they find life unless I am willing to give them the freedom to pursue their own dreams and desires?

There is no life in suffocated dreams.

What kind of life can you find with a heart that has no feelings? What are they left with if they surrender to my attempts to manage their lives? How can they pursue life without risking pain and disappointment in their efforts?

What am I to do with their dreams?

As my children make their choices and I stay engaged with them, encouraging them as they do, I suffer with them in their pain and share in their disappointment, as I am their father. And I am faced with another question. It is difficult enough for me to bear my own pain and disappointment but...

How am I to bear their pain and disappointment as well?

Put your heart into it
My older daughter Jessica loves animals. When she was ten she taught a stray cat to sit, stay, and come on command. Then she wanted a German Shepherd. I said no. She asked me many times. I said no, not once, but many times. She is a very persistent young woman.

Then we went on a family camping trip. She wanted to go horseback riding; so I took her.

Big mistake.

When we returned home from our vacation she wanted a horse. We owned a wooded lot with no place to keep a horse, but that does not deter a young dreamer. She began to search the classified ads and read about the horses for sale. She would clip the adds, take them into the large field that bordered our property and sit in the tall grass and dream of having a horse.

Sometimes she would call and talk to the seller. It irritated me. She wasn't getting a horse. She had no money. We had no place for a horse. She was only fourteen. It was simply unreasonable.

Her persistence in asking the question and my rejection and dismissal of something that was absolutely impossible brought her to tears many times in the following years.

Some dreams are not only unreasonable, they are impossible. Not all dreams come true nor should they. Certainly an unreasonable, impossible dream like having a horse was not meant to come true.

Finally, as a method to find some relief from her relentless questioning about getting a horse, I told her that she could talk to me about a horse when she had two thousand dollars.

Did I tell you she had no money and no job, and was fourteen?

Within twelve months my daughter had found several jobs and had saved eighteen hundred dollars and I knew that I was in serious trouble!

When she learned how much it would cost to clear our woods and fence a pasture for the horse (she had looked up and called the contractors to get bids) she found that the neighbors were happy for her to keep her horse in their empty fenced pasture with a small building for animals. And she was able to find some people who simply wanted someone to take care of a twenty-year-old horse that had belonged to their daughter. My daughter would simply be required to buy the feed and pay any vets bills. She was able to get her horse, a place to keep it, and still had the eighteen hundred dollars left for feed and care.

I don't know how these desires came to be within my children. It confuses me. Sometimes it irritates me. And sometimes I think their dreams frighten me.

Why am I afraid? Why do their dreams threaten me? Why have I put so much energy into trying to dissuade them, or divert them?

Dreams of redemption

My son wanted to get a motorcycle when I purchased my Harley. If he had wanted a Harley, it may have been easier for me, but he wanted a sport bike—one of those bikes that many young men his age are killed on each year.

I didn't think it was such a good idea. I was certainly afraid of what could happen, but was also concerned because frankly, he couldn't afford it. He was a young man out on his own, and there wasn't much I could say and little I could do. I will let Matthew, my son, tell you his story in his own words.

I did mention that to you that not all dreams are meant to come true, and many only lead to disappointment didn't I?

"Since I was a young boy, I had dreamed of owning my very own sport bike motorcycle. The attraction and freedom of a motorcycle is one very few people get to truly appreciate and experience; but for those of us who do, the theft of a bike is a very personal violation of our privacy and lives.

In May of 2004, after waiting two months for the bike that I had ordered, my dream had finally come true. Unfortunately, in mid-June, I had some issues with the engine."

Allow me to interrupt him here and say that the "issues" happened on the return trip from visiting his future wife in Eastern Washington when he failed to negotiate a corner. He rode his bike off the road and into a newly plowed field, where he discovered a rock that threw him from the bike and busted the case of his engine. He was not hurt, but his new motorcycle now required an engine rebuild. I'll let him resume his story.

"These troubles started a long and tiring process of rebuilding my dream, literally from the ground up. On August 18, 2004, after two months of working to repair the engine, I finally restored my dream back to "brand new," along with the addition of a handful of custom parts that made this machine a true extension of who I am, making it one of a kind. The following day I rode to work, excited to be living my dream again and anxious to get back to enjoying the summer weather. When I arrived, I was careful to use the bike's built-in handle bar lock and after-market wheel lock—a practice that I had established from day one to protect my bike. This disables the motorcycle from being ridden and makes it very difficult to move. After putting in an honest day's work, I clocked out, grabbed my gear to head home, only to find that the bike I had parked and locked up only ten feet away from the rear entrance of the building where I worked was nowhere to be seen. Someone had stolen my bike in broad daylight. This was to be the beginning of a nightmare that has affected every aspect of my life for the last two-and-a-half years."

My son's account of the story was taken from an excerpt of the letter he wrote to the judge at the sentencing of the thief that had taken my son's motorcycle. My son's dream did not turn out at all the way that he thought it would. Not many dreams do.

Dreams are dangerous.

There simply is no "happily ever after" for us in the here and now of this life. And there is no guarantee where a dream might take you.

For my dream, I had pondered owning my Harley for over twelve years. It had taken five years before I had the courage to admit to myself that someday I would like to own a Harley, and three more years before I could admit it out loud. I simply wasn't sure it was okay for me to even dream about such a thing.

I suppose my dream began when I was twelve, and my dad purchased a Honda 90 trail bike. It was on this bike that I learned to ride, do wheelies, spin donuts, and go so fast that the water would stream from my eyes toward my ears. Perhaps this was the genesis of my dream of owning a Harley?

Or possibly it was birthed in my dad who, years before I was born owned a Matchless 650 and would take my mother for rides. (He said he sold it because he thought mom would kill herself on it.) Maybe mine was a dream I captured from the heart of my dad?

To my surprise, when my children learned of my dream, they became my biggest supporters. I explained to them many times why I couldn't just go get a Harley. I simply didn't have the money, it wasn't the right time, there were other expenses we needed to take care of, and my list went on.

During one such conversation, I remember telling my daughter as I walked her back from feeding her horse one evening that if I bought a Harley it would ruin my dream. The dream would then become the maintenance of oil changes, mechanical issues, making sure the air pressure was correct in the tires, and keeping it clean.

These would only ruin my dream, I explained to her.

I know. It was a lame argument, but it provided me the safety of the familiar. I did not have to face the chaos of the dream like my son had faced in the pursuit of his dream. And I was avoiding the risk of letting it take me into the unknown where I might get hurt.

My wife has since purchased her own horse and I did purchase my Harley. We have had issues with both the horse and the Harley, but in putting action to our dreams we have been discovering things about ourselves that had been lost in the confusion of raising our family. It was the right thing for us to wait until the family was older—spending life with our children as they grew and pursuing the dream of family. And it was the right thing to let ourselves "dream" when we did.

It has been in our pursuit of dreams that life has continued for us, blossomed if you will, as our hearts have discovered deeper joys and found greater liberation from the suffocation of the well managed safety of "proper living."

I am not sure how it has happened, but God has given me permission to dream that I had somehow lost on my way to becoming an adult and young father. In the process, I am discovering my heart with new eyes and better understanding who I am. Strangely enough, in my effort to pursue dreams, my family and even friends have found an invitation to pursue their own dreams and discover their hearts in the process as well.

Finding the permission to dream, discovering this window into my heart and the subsequent insights of who I am as a person are not without confusion and disappointment, as my son came to find out. There is a good deal of risk in this business of dreams, and I can find no way to avoid the pain of it. These dream ventures and explorations have been helpful in assisting me in my pursuit of life, but they do not always lead to a happy ending. Nor do dreams always come true.

They do invite me to open my heart to living and feeling, and afford me the opportunity to experience the glory of life. If I never reach for a dream I am left simply wearing out the springs in my recliner. If I never reach for a dream how will I ever make a new discovery of life?

I have found freedom to dream, but what do I do with these dreams? They are messy—confusing at best. I am afraid of the exposure and the risk of pursuing them, regardless of the benefit. They simply are not safe.

What do I do?

Four

Do Something Disease

"Christians have often disputed as to whether what leads the Christian home is good actions or Faith in Christ...It does seem to me like asking which blade in a pair of scissors is most necessary. A serious moral effort is the only thing that will bring you to the point where you throw in the towel. Faith in Christ is the only thing to save you from despair at that point: and out of the Faith in Him, good actions must inevitably come." —C.S. Lewis

I want to earn it

I have heard people say to me that they need to "get their life together," which means to me a life that is collected, organized, purpose driven, and integrated. I think having a life that is together is a very good thing.

That is what I want too.

I've already mentioned that I've spent a good deal of effort and time trying to be good and subsequently to "get my life together." My attempts have included reading the *Seven*

Habits of Highly Successful People, by Steven Covey. I want to be a Highly Successful People. I have gained some good insights for my effort, but I don't think that I am yet in the "highly successful" category.

I've worked through *The Purpose Driven Life,* by Rick Warren and discovered some helpful principles. I've heard about the various twelve step programs and know many people who have found great benefit from working through those steps. I have come across numerous other programs, multi-step plans and teaching aids that have been designed to help me get my life organized and together, purpose driven and integrated.

Most of them have very good ideas and useful principles. Many of the steps have served to help people on their journeys to greater personal discovery and have proven to be very useful in helping them "get their lives together."

I already know that if I were to be measured on a "goodness" scale, I simply would not rank all that high. Perhaps I'm simply poor at following directions because in spite of all my effort to follow the programs and various steps, I still have not been able to gain the sense of being "together" that the programs promised me.

I have tried really hard, and sometimes I feel that I am simply grasping at whatever seems to offer me a ray of hope for the life I want. Sometimes my effort is nothing short of frantic—sometimes. Other times I get plain tired of it all and simply give up, only to find the thirst becomes more than I can bear, and once again I find myself doing something, anything that might help me to find and discover life.

I find that I am still driven by a sense that there is something more, something that is missing in my life, and if I could only discover what it is, then I could fix it. I just don't know the formula to find the answer. There must be something to satisfy this nagging sense that there really is a better life. It is like a puzzle and if I could just figure out the secret code or the magic steps then I'd find the life I so desperately want. Then I could be satisfied.

And so I do something.

Sometimes it really doesn't matter the "what" or the "something" that I do. The doing may not make any sense whatsoever, but at least I'm doing something. Most of the time the something doesn't get me any closer to my goal of finding life, it's really like driving the other direction simply because there is no traffic in that direction, but it makes me feel as if I'm going somewhere because I'm moving!

This "doing something" seems to be woven into the very fabric of my human nature. It is most helpful when I can aim the "doing" at a specific "something," but as I said, I don't find that to be necessary. I simply need to be doing the "something." The doing makes me feel better, even if I'm not making any progress toward my goal.

I suppose it is a part of the universal merit system—we try to earn what we want and so we do the "something" that we believe will earn it for us.

I work at earning what I want all the time.

I've learned and have been taught this merit system over and over again in my lifetime. This system has been taught and maintained in the codes of societies throughout time. We learn what we must do to earn what we want.

Santa gives gifts to the children who have been good all year. We earn the gifts by our good behavior. They are the reward for being good all year long. In school, grades were the reward for studying, applying yourself to the assignment, learning the content, passing the tests. Good grades were earned. Passing to the next grade was earned as well. Sometimes there was special recognition for exceptional work. If I didn't perform well, it meant failure and possibly being held back.

When I started working, the same rules applied, if I would work hard at my job, show up on time and do a little bit extra, the chances were better for earning a raise and again, possible advancement. If I work hard at my marriage, remember anniversaries and birthdays, treat my wife with consideration and compassion, putting her interests ahead of mine, I expect my marriage to be rewarded for my *good efforts.*

It's doing things the old fashioned way

—earning them.

A good system

As I work hard, applying myself to this merit system, doing something where I can earn what I want to earn helps me to live an organized and purposeful life. It is appropriate to put effort into life, whether in my education, my job, my hobby, my marriage, parenting, or whatever I find myself doing. I should perform the things I do with the intention of doing my best, using the skill and creativity given to me. It is always a good thing.

Always.

In general, things will turn out better for me when I do.

But failure is not a bad thing either. Failure helps to teach me the skills and abilities I have and the ones I don't have. Failure gives me insight to help me choose the things I would like to work harder at—the areas to which I might apply myself to improve my performance.

It really is a pretty good system.

It is a system that I can understand and I can comprehend the consequences of not applying it myself. Bad things will happen to me that I will not enjoy if I do not pay my bills on time, if I do not show up for work, if I spend all of my money on habits, or if I ignore my wife and children to pursue my own interests.

I've learned I don't want to face the unpleasant consequences of not applying myself to doing what is right and good. I do not enjoy the consequences that only add to the chaos and confusion in my life. I've learned by working hard to manage my life, there is less confusion, and not as much chaos. My efforts are rewarded by less frustration and a bit more order.

So I listen to the *Seven Habits* and the *Purpose Driven Life* programs and use them to arrange and organize myself. I use all that I've learned about working hard and apply the ideas so that I might earn what I want and avoid the consequences of what I don't want.

I'm searching to find life, satisfaction, enjoyment, and fulfillment.

When I pause to listen to myself, when I shush the noise of everything attempting to capture my attention, this is the basic desire I find within me. It is as if it has been written inside of me, on the fabric of my heart, and I can't erase it. It is only logical then that I would use the "doing" that I've learned which rewards me in the rest of my life to apply myself to the "something" that will help me reach this goal of finding life. It all seems very straight forward and simple enough.

Why wouldn't I be able to apply the rules of organizing my life to my efforts to find life?

My problem is that all of my "doing" doesn't always work to get me closer to the "something" I want. I am busy doing and I know I am moving but I get the general feeling I am driving the wrong direction, getting further from where I really want to be and moving away from what I want the most.

It is frustrating.

What I've come to understand is that my goal is to find life, not earn a wage or some type of advancement. The rules of the merit system that I've learned throughout my life simply do not apply to my effort to find life. In all of my attempts to try to earn the life I want, my efforts seem to work more against me than for me.

And the harder I try the farther away I find I am from the life that I want.

I'm coming to the conclusion that if God has designed me for Him and for His pleasure, then that is where I must look to find the life I want so much—in the relationship which is part of my very design. The closer I can be to Him, then the more I will know the life that I have been working so hard to find; and finding that relationship and knowing the pleasure of God is not something to be earned or maintained by this merit system I have learned.

Glimpses of life

I have had a few moments, ever so fleeting when my thirst for life has been briefly satisfied. These were not self-realization moments or a time where I found answers to all of my questions or suddenly, with the alignment of the planets or the synchronization of all the traffic lights leading me to the last parking spot on the street, that my problems had resolved and everything was right with the world.

I have no reason that I can offer you to explain the cause of these moments. Somehow, the chaos and confusion of my life was briefly interrupted when all seemed right for me and life was good, complete in spite of all my personal turmoil. Just then, for a few brief minutes and for some unknown reason, I found a place of rich contentment and confidence that all was well, a sense that I was at least moving in the general direction of finding the life I wanted.

One of these occasions I remember was leaning on the wood rail of the deck at the house we had built. It was a dream house for me, one I had imagined living in when I was a teenager. I stood there on my deck looking into the woods, at the yard and the property we lived on, feeling very satisfied with my life and the work of my hands.

Just to be clear, I had plenty of issues with my life right then. There were unfinished projects that needed my attention. The annoying list of routine chores of household maintenance was growing even as I stood there. There was a good deal of tension in my job as the demands continued to increase and the demands of my job didn't care that my wife and I were raising three teenagers, and these three teenagers with their raging hormones and emerging independence provided me with more chaos and confusion than I ever wanted to deal with.

This was not a moment where life had resolved for me as the progression of chords will at the end of a good song or in the ending of a good movie where the good prevails and love flourishes. The natural state of my life is one with a constant level of tension never seeming to fully resolve.

Yet for some reason, for a few brief moments the tension seemed to be subdued by the inner-strength of gratitude and satisfaction. The demands and chaos of my life were not able to overcome the simple pleasure of standing on my deck looking into the woods and enjoying the peace of the moment.

It was my "moment," right then; this place where I stood— life right now, one moment that still holds for me a deep sense of satisfaction and fulfillment. A moment that I have looked back on many times wishing I could recapture it, wishing I knew what I could do to repeat it.

I remember another moment riding mountain bikes with my brothers, following them on a trail through the woods, and Tim, the middle brother of us three, attempting to pass Kev, the youngest. Tim took off to the side, attempting to get to the narrow opening that dropped a foot or so as it passed between two old-growth trees. Kev was unwilling to concede to Tim's aggressive attempt to pass, and both of them met where the path narrowed between the trees. They were left with no option but to try and squeeze through the narrow opening side by side, going over exposed roots, launching themselves and their bicycles into the air, hoping to land where the trail continued below the roots. They both fell once they landed on the downhill side of the path. We all laughed as we collected ourselves to continue our ride.

The next day I was in the lead, entering the same section of trail. A Tim is a Tim as Kev and I will say, and once again he attempted the same pass on me. The results were the same as we met at the restriction between the two trees, and side by side we once again launched ourselves into the air. This time, Tim and I bumped shoulders in the air (And Tim yelled at me for being reckless!). We both landed on our wheels continuing down the trail but the mid air bump surprised us both so much we simply fell over and the three of us laughed until we were too tired to laugh any more.

For me, it was a simple moment filled with life, a celebration as pure as any I have ever experienced. It was a moment that happened upon me by accident and one that could not have been planned or repeated if I were to try.

I love those moments. As I said, there have been others as well. Like the Christmas when I gave my wife her first diamond ring and gave my kids pictures I had made for them. These are precious moments to me, filled with gratitude and deeply satisfying.

I wish I could somehow relive them. I wish I could rewind and replay that moment in time and relive the experience. I wish I could capture them so I could somehow hold the sheer delight and celebration they offered, but I can only attempt to remember by putting the moment to story and repeating it to those who were with me, hoping to relive just a little of the pleasure.

The memory of those moments all too quickly fades as the onslaught of daily life and the responsibilities I face replaces them with the seemingly endless routines and the frustration which often accompanies what I know as life. I love those moments, and it seems the harder I try to create them the more unobtainable they become.

I love the glimpses they have left me with. They tease me when I remember them. I sometimes wonder what life might be like if I could only "do something" to live more of these moments. What can I do to achieve the life and the satisfaction that I want?

How can I experience more of these moments where everything seems so right?

I keep trying, but the routine seems to be winning. I fight against the monotony of seemingly endless days and the feeling of futility that grows as weeks quickly turn to months, and the months turn into years faster than they ought to. The years have added up to numbers that I couldn't even imagine as a kid just a few short years ago.

If I can't earn the life that I want then what can I do to change my life?

As hard as I try there seems to be nothing I can do.

I really want to get it right
The world has an order to it. Night and Day have their time and place. They are predicable and dependable. Rain falls on the mountains forming rivers that return the water to the sea where it evaporates to repeat the process one more time. On its journey the water nourishes the plants and animals. These are all part of the natural order.

We also live in a created social order. A red light at the intersection means stop, green means go. In the US we drive on the right side of the road, we do not pass when there is a solid yellow line on our side of the road. We have building codes originally intended to make the buildings safe. There are electrical communication standards that enable one device to "talk" to another. If the standards are not followed, things crash, the order is broken, and things no longer work.

It is very beneficial to have systems. A system provides an order from which everyone can build upon. The system defines the "right" way to do things.

I really want to have my place in the world. I want to feel like I make a contribution to the order and purpose of making things work. I do not want to be irrelevant or a screw up or be a loser. I want to help things work so the system keeps working.

I want to do things right.

If I can only get it right, then maybe I can find my place and will know I am making my contribution. I will be a vital part of helping the system to work and maybe even a part of helping the system to work better. Not only will I be able to participate in the order and purpose of life, but I will then be able to let other people know the right and proper way to live so that they might be able to get it right too.

And so, once again I set about the doing. Working very hard to do whatever will help me earn my place and feel I am a part—that I belong. Working to capture a moment where I feel alive.

There is great benefit to having this order in life, a right and proper method to organize and arrange things. When I spend my energy fighting this order it is akin to fighting gravity, in the end it is a futile effort. And so I work at doing it right, to capture that feeling, that moment where I am alive. Surely if I do the right thing, in the right way then it must be good and I will be good because I am doing the right things.

In my efforts to achieve "good" I have worked very hard at learning about the system God designed so I might do things the "right" way and behave the "proper" way. I even began to list the things the Bible said I should be doing and the things I shouldn't be doing so that I could be right, convinced if I do things right, life will work out for me.

In my study of the Bible, I found many commands and things it said I should do, all good and very useful in guiding me toward the life I want. But I found once again, I became obsessed with doing. I am afraid I simply can't help it. And when I found it was impossible for me to do what the Bible was commanding me to do, I reasoned the Bible must mean something slightly different than my understanding. I reasoned it must mean for me to do the something that I *can* do and not the something that is impossible for me to do.

Why else would it command me to be perfect if I couldn't be perfect?

So I worked very hard at being perfect and redefined perfection as something I could do.

I really want get it right and to be good.

I don't have to earn it

It was Jesus who said, "I came so that they can have real and eternal life, more and better life than they ever dreamed of."
—The Message, John 10:10

That is what I've dreamed about. It is the life for which I've been searching all this time. My throat gets dry as I ponder how good this life could be. As you might imagine, I really like the sound of this.

I might be beyond help. I still want to earn it. I still find myself looking for the strategy that will help me to be good enough, looking for the plan that will lead me to the great accomplishment of life. I want to do something. Anything. It's not that I'm ungrateful or don't appreciate it, I simply want to pull my weight, to do my part, to pay my way.

I've worked hard to learn the rules and work within the system. I've applied myself to being good and doing the right things. My problem is that I do not have the strength or ability to be good enough to earn this life that I want to live, the life that I am looking for. There is no program, plan or strategy I can apply to achieve it. When I look honestly at the commands I've been given, I fail in even the smallest of deeds to be good enough.

I am ashamed.

I simply can't do the "somethings" that the Bible talks about.

Slowly I am admitting I can't do what I need to, but I am unsure and even afraid to abandon this merit system that I've learned. I know I am not all that good. I also know that all my best effort has not rewarded me with the life I want, but what I've gained is better than when I lived only to serve my addictions and fears.

I know and have been told I can't earn it, but it doesn't stop me from trying. I still want to. Perhaps it is only my stubborn pride refusing to let go of doing something to earn it.

Jesus said He came to give me the life that I long for.

A gift.

Gifts are given. They cannot be earned by doing the "somethings."

Trying to earn a gift is an offense to the giver, but old habits die hard for me and to simply believe I've been given the gift I want so much is simply unbelievable.

Besides, what am I supposed to do? Surely I am supposed to do something.

I am supposed to be obedient, right?

And then I read, "Be still and know that I am God,"[3] and once again I am afraid of the inactivity and silence. All I can see is my failure. I have fallen far short of the aim. These systems are useless in helping me to find life and only serve my pride.

What I really need is to learn how to follow Him.

Five

How Am I Doing?

"A noble man compares himself by an idea which is higher than himself; and a mean man, by one lower than himself. The one produces aspiration; the other ambition, which is the way in which a vulgar man aspires."

–Henry Ward Beecher

We are not in this alone

Graduating into the seventh grade only added to my growing sense of insecurity and increased the amount of chaos I felt as I entered into the early years of adolescence. Grade school had been a one room, one teacher event, which changed once a year, and only after meeting the requirements to graduate into the next grade. Now there were seven classes a day with as many different teachers, music being one of the seven. Music was a required class with one choice; choir or band; sing or play.

As I considered the two options, it became apparent that to choose band and play an instrument required another decision. I would have to choose from a number of cumbersome, and in my mind, not very cool wind instruments. (From my recollection, the only choices offered were wind instruments such as trumpet, saxophone, trombone, etc. Guitars were too modern and I do not remember any other string instruments as choices. Drums were cool but there were no openings for more drummers.) It simply compounded the complexity of what was already a very traumatic adjustment. It was one more decision adding to the chaos. What is the right choice? Which one is best? What do I want to do?

More confusion.

As I weighed out my options, the decision became rather simple for me. Choir presented the simpler choice. One decision. No instrument to carry to class. No required practicing at home. Nothing to forget. Simply show up for class each day and sing. Much easier. Less complicated.

I expected choir to be an easier class than English and math. It shouldn't be too difficult to earn a passing grade, as half of the grade was showing up, and the ability to sing was not a requirement.

I could do this. And my vocal efforts would be masked by the mass of voices in the room singing with me. All I had to do was keep my lips moving with the other voices and not make any disturbing sounds and I would be fine.

For several weeks it was all working out as I had hoped and planned it would. Then the music teacher that I thought was going to be easy to get along with dropped the bomb on us—

the one hidden requirement of the class she had neglected to include in the class summary when I was considering my options. She had kept it to herself, hidden as it were, until that moment.

In order to earn the easy passing grade I was counting on, each of us, one at a time, would be required to go to the front of the class and sing the part we had learned in class. The sopranos, the altos, the tenors, and the basses would all sing their parts.

Alone.

No other voices to hide behind or parts to blend with.

No other voices to follow or use as a queue for my part.

No supporting music.

All by myself.

In front of the class.

She called it a solo.

As I listened to her announce this unanticipated and unreasonable requirement, my stomach began to knot up and my head began to spin. Without looking around the room to check, I had a sense this same nervous feeling was spreading through the rest of the class like a bad smell. As I was making a new acquaintance with anxiety and apprehension, I realized we would be spending a good amount of time together, as the due date for my assigned solo was to be several weeks into the future.

Clearly I had made the wrong choice.

I tried to ignore the growing anxiety as the weeks passed and then, just as my dreaded dentist appointment, the day arrived well before it was welcome. The choir teacher, Ms. Ford proudly announced it was time for each of us to sing our solos—the music we had learned over the past weeks. I received an ever so slight reprieve when the she asked for volunteers.

"What are you, nuts?" I thought to myself. "Who in their right mind would volunteer to stand in front of this group, waiting for the inevitable public humiliation?"

"I'll go." One of the sopranos offered raising her hand.

"Unbelievable!" I thought to myself. Then it occurred to me I just might be able to dodge this one if she left it to a volunteer assignment. It was a faint and insecure hope, but it was hope.

Maybe we would run out of time?

Maybe the teacher would come to the realization that listening to a group of seventh graders sing was a misguided assignment and then repent and change her mind?

Maybe she would get married and move away?

And maybe the world would end and Jesus would come back before my public humiliation?

I was grasping for any way out, and there was no chance of a snowball in a very hot place that I was going to raise my hand to be the next volunteer.

And so I sat and waited. I sat quietly with my fear and a fading faint hope within me, as I desperately considered how I might find some way to avoid the assignment.

I waited.

And waited.

I sat on my hands when necessary to make sure she did not mistake any movement on my part to be an indication that I was interested in volunteering to sing.

This may have been my first exposure to the law of diminishing options; each day that passed left only one path ahead of me, until there was only one option.

It was my turn to sing.

I don't remember hearing the words from Ms. Ford's mouth, and I don't remember getting up from my seat. I don't remember walking to the front of the class or stepping up to the lectern where I would have to face an audience of my peers. I had confidence I could sing my part with the group, but was completely unsure of myself alone. I wasn't even sure if I could coax anything from my mouth even if I knew how to move my lips.

Was this the end for me?

Would I freeze with fear?

Would I even be able to make a sound?

Would it even sound like music?

Over the weeks I had listened to my classmates sing their solos. Several of them, I concluded, had made the wrong choice just as I had, and should have chosen band instead of choir. They simply couldn't carry a tune, and it was embarrassing to hear their effort.

I took a deep breath and looking at the lectern in front of me I timidly began to sing my assigned part. Desperate to make a sound and not screw it up too badly, I pressed on, waiting for it to be over and done with. Soon I would be back in my chair and this too would be past.

Maybe having friends wasn't all that important?

Maybe the humiliation wouldn't get too far outside of the classroom?

After what seemed like an eternity, I came to the end. Relieved it was over, I began to brace myself for the obligatory comments from my teacher so I could take my chair.

"Very well done Steve! You have a very nice voice!"

The words held within them surprise and delight! And there was no small amount of surprise in me as well, as I considered what she was saying. Then a few of the girls in class complimented me on my voice as well.

I was stunned; astonished; dumbfounded.

How did this happen? I had braced myself for the inevitable subdued laughter and quiet ridicule, but it didn't happen. I only received congratulations and encouragement.

I don't remember much else of choir in that, my seventh year of school. I do remember at the end of the year as we were presented the choices for the eight year of school, I chose choir. I sang in junior high and continued singing into my high school years. It was an easy class and an easy grade. Since then, I've volunteered to sing in other choirs and vocal groups. I have even sung solos more times than I can count, and on a few occasions in front of hundreds of people.

Somewhere along the way, I found I really enjoy singing. Anxiety and apprehension have simply joined me, in some ways they've become friends in the journey. Today they serve to help me prepare, but never to look for a way out. The choice is now mine and not an assignment. I sing because I want to. The music gives voice to a part of me I don't yet fully understand, a voice to an inner part of me that requires more than the simple definitions that words in a sentence can offer.

And the courage to sing is due in large part because Ms. Ford and a few of my classmates paid me a compliment. And then someone else reinforced it.

As a skinny, sixty-pound seventh grader, I didn't believe I could sing, and I inadvertently put myself in a situation where I had no other choice. As a result, I discovered something new about myself.

Comparing—the search for validation

Perhaps it's just me, but I've spent more time than I want to admit during my life searching for affirmation, attempting to find in myself that ability or talent that would validate me as a person and give a sense of purpose to my existence. If you would have questioned me as a teenager I would not have been able to put words to my search. I couldn't have explained it to you at the time, but affirmation and validation was the gift Ms. Ford gave me that year in seventh grade choir with her compliments.

I was validated by my teacher and by my peers, and it was through their gift I discovered I could sing.

I confess I have spent more of my life wrestling with insecurity than I have with overconfidence. When I discovered I could sing it offered me a morsel of confidence. With confidence I continued singing. As I practiced and learned techniques and vocal quality I found myself listening and critiquing others who would sing, then comparing myself to their ability.

Did their breathing interrupt the melody? Did they enunciate properly? How was their pitch?

Many times I found myself thinking I could do better. "*Oh too bad, they missed that note,*" or "*They should not have taken a breath right there. They should know better than that!"* Then there were those who excelled well beyond my abilities, and I was left both impressed and insecure after listening to their talent.

I admit my critical evaluation of another singer, comparing how I would do in the same situation is a bit judgmental, and yes, even arrogant. Yet even as I try to quit making comparisons, no matter how hard I try, I simply am unable to stop comparing.

Sometimes I've felt guilty for comparing myself. I've been told we shouldn't compare. In fact, I expect I have told others they shouldn't compare themselves as well, playing the hypocrite, I admit. I think comparing is simply part and parcel of the human experience.

We all do it.

I'm not trying to convince you comparing is an honorable or good thing to do, or offer you an excuse for the comparing I do. I am saying it is what we do with almost everything we find to do, almost everything in which more than two people have an interest, we compare.

I'm not sure what it is I hope to gain by comparing myself with someone else, perhaps the satisfaction of superiority? Perhaps I am hoping for further validation of my own abilities or proving my own worth?

Whatever the motivation, I have found that in my comparing I am never satisfied with being better than another and always find there is someone much better than me. Comparing never seems to provide the validation or the satisfaction of an improved sense of self-worth. And rarely do others agree with my assessment, so there is more risk than gain from open comparison, unless of course the other person is equally attempting to belittle the person under critique.

If you are still unsure of how much we compare ourselves with each other, consider our competition for a moment. Competition is the most obvious engagement in the pastime of comparing that we participate in. We compete to see who is the best, who is the fastest, who is the biggest, who is the most accurate, and the list is unending.

We compete at almost everything we do.

We have billion dollar industries designed around and for the pleasure of competition; the Super Bowl, March Madness, the World Series, Wimbledon, The Masters, NASCAR, the list is endless.

We can't own a pet without comparing them. Someone buys a dog, and then someone else buys the same kind of dog, and before you know it there are judges, an obstacle course, a ring or a race track to determine the best. We have cat shows, rabbit shows, horse shows, rodeo and livestock shows. We compare the looks, the build, the speed, or the agility of the animals, and then we compare the behavior.

We grow flowers and have shows to select the best. We compare our jobs, the houses we own, the cars we drive and the lawns we manicure, and then we compete by judging the best house, or the fastest riding lawnmower—some going so far as to convert the mower into racing machines, competing and comparing to see which is the fastest and who is the best. We even compete in our recreation, from boating to bird watching. We compete to compare our efforts and determine who is the fastest, the prettiest, the strongest, the tallest, and the all-around best.

It seems there is nothing we do that doesn't involve comparison. What is it driving this irresistible urge to compare everything we do?

What is it that I am competing for? Confidence? Competence? Validation?

I've played sports and gave my all in an effort to win the big prize. I have concluded when my view of myself depends upon how well I do in competition, it usually only leaves me discouraged. I may do okay and find a few moments of glory, but if I compare myself with those who excel like Tiger Woods or Michael Jordon, I find myself wanting to give up. I can never measure up. I am not able to compete with what they have individually accomplished.

There are a number of reasons why I don't measure up to that standard. My history and my origins are radically different from theirs. I don't share the resources they had available to them. My time and place were completely different from their time and place with different pressures and a different environment. If I insist on comparing myself to them, I only find myself inferior. I cannot compete. The playing field is not equal, and in their league I cannot even be a competent loser.

This competing and comparison is a double-edged sword. In seventh grade, it boosted my confidence and changed my life as I was compared to the other singers in my choir. But when I compare myself with those who have superior talents and capabilities, I am left with no gratification, no recognition.

It leaves me feeling irrelevant and unnoticed, lost in a crowd of nameless faces, insignificant and unimportant.

Criticism is not a spiritual gift

If you are thinking my effort to gain some self-respect or notoriety by constantly comparing myself to others is much like spitting into the wind, well I agree with you wholeheartedly. None-the-less I am still driven to prove my own worth, to find a place where I am competent and can separate myself from the disregarded and insignificant. Because I cannot compete with those who seem to have achieved success and significance, I have found an inclination to trade my efforts to compete for trite criticism of those who can compete where I cannot.

I find it much easier to evaluate and assess the inabilities of others. This seems to come naturally for me, and it is so much easier than honestly evaluating myself.

All I have to do is critique the efforts of those who are attempting to gain the very same approval I seek. And when I scrutinize the efforts of someone else, it helps for me to level my criticism with confidence, pretending if necessary, I know what I'm talking about. Over time and with practice I get better, learning the subtleties of the sport or art I am judging, and then making my arrogant assessments with confidence to sound as if I know what I am talking about. The more I learn about the sport or event I want to judge, the better my criticism's sounds.

There is one minor problem with this. To stand apart and judge means that I am now out of the game. I have removed myself from the possibility of ever winning the ribbon or gaining the notoriety or achieving the significance I was competing for. If I elevate myself to judge, the award can only be given to one of those willing to compete.

Are my gifts and talents so insignificant that I cannot participate and glory in my successes and acknowledge my failures?

How do I learn to enjoy my abilities and talents—the things that I can do?

Why should I even compete if there is no hope of me winning?

I wrestle with these questions. And I wonder what might happen if those in the world of sports took the same approach. There would be no Super Bowl, no Masters Golf tournament, or World Series, because no one would compete.

Maybe winning is the goal, but perhaps it is not really the point? Maybe the point is found in the test of the competition where each competitor is not only measured but they are offered the discovery of their strengths and abilities? Maybe it is more for the individual to understand themselves than it is for the display to the crowds? What is certain is there will be no determination of abilities and skills without the challenge of competition. It is in competing that both the spectators and the participants discover the talents and character of the competitors as revealed by the test.

It is widely agreed Tiger Woods is currently the best golfer in the sport. Maybe the best we'll ever see. It is the competition that reveals his abilities, and it is only in the testing of competition that anyone, including Tiger, can know how good he really is.

In some way, Tiger is only as good *as* his competition. If Tiger played golf by himself, if everyone conceded that he was the best and no one ever showed up to compete because they concluded that they are not as good, Tiger would never be challenged. He would never be under pressure. There would be no reason to labor over a thirty-foot double-breaking putt, or a two-hundred-thirty yard shot from behind a tree that must fly the water to land on the green. We would never know how good he is, because he would never be challenged by the abilities of the other players. And *he* would never know how good he is, because he would never be tested by the competition.

He needs the competition to test him so that he can learn, and display, and use his talent.

If competition is going to teach me about myself then there must be a competitor with whom I can compare myself and my abilities. There must be at least two who are willing to challenge their God given abilities and talents to offer their best in measuring themselves against the other. To discover who, on this day, is the best.

If we can't really know about ourselves without comparison, then comparison and competition are part and parcel of the life we have been given to live. However there is also a very serious caution to be given about using comparison and competition even when I *don't* use it as a means to "win" my approval and achieve the significance I want.

The caution is not in losing. Even Tiger Woods has lost and lost badly to unknown golfers. And there have been times that he has fallen just short of the prize as well as the times when he has won and won big. On any given day the test or the challenge might prove another to be better, even better than the best. Even the best will fail the test occasionally as the test reveals more of the limits of their talents and abilities.

For some unknown reason I grew up thinking that Jesus was the best at everything and could do anything.

I mean, He did a lot of pretty cool things, spitting in the eyes of a blind guy so he could see again, telling demons where to go and watching them run, telling people who couldn't walk to get up and leave, walking on water, and even bringing dead people back to life.

Pretty amazing.

Then I began to wonder.

Could Jesus beat Tiger Woods in a game of golf?

Think about the question for a moment with me.

There are many talented golfers. Many of the professionals can crush a drive beyond and to a point on the course that most of the rest of us can only dream about on a golf course.

But could Jesus beat Tiger Woods?

At first I thought yes. Of course Jesus could beat Tiger Woods. But then I had to consider whether Jesus could line up on the defensive line of a professional football league and drive the offensive linemen to his backside to take on the blocking running back to get to the quarterback. In order to accomplish such a feat, He would have to outperform everyone else in the game. If I thought Jesus could beat Tiger Woods simply because He is Jesus, then he would also have to be able to take to the field and outplay any professional football or baseball player, then onto the ice and play or fight hockey better than any hockey player. He would have to have the ability to best every athlete in every sport.

It would be humanly impossible.

So back to my question: Could Jesus beat Tiger Woods?

I don't think so.

I think Jesus gave Tiger a gift, a father and a place in time that we are able to witness and enjoy as we watch him play the game with greatness.

I am not Tiger Woods. I am a different man with different gifts and talents that have come from my inheritance, my background, and my time in history. And I get to appreciate Tiger's abilities while I learn to enjoy my own, living out my time and place in history.

If I never compete or compare myself, I may never discover my abilities or talents, but I cannot use competition and comparison to validate myself. It will always lead me to despair and take me out of the game, which is likely to then lead me into criticism and blame, because I can always find someone else better.

The dark side of comparing

There is another side of comparing that is to be taken very seriously. There is good reason so many have shunned competition and instructed us not to compare ourselves with others, but as I have tried to demonstrate, it is impossible for us to stop comparing. Athletics may be the most prevalent example, but we compare at almost everything.

The dark side of comparing has to do with the irrelevant, the insignificant and the discarded. When I test myself or compare myself and conclude myself to be superior to another, due to my abilities or looks or intelligence or whatever, and then I elevate myself above them, at least in my own mind I have chosen a dark and evil path. There are differences among us, but when I begin to think of you as irrelevant and discard you, it demeans you and robs you of the dignity and respect you deserve as a person.

In my school years, there were several kids I would have described as bullies. They were bigger than I was and tougher and meaner, in my estimation. But my distaste for them did not deter me from treating other kids with the same contempt when I decided myself to be superior to them.

This dark side of comparing and competition is the side that leads me to believing I am superior to and above another. Comparison leaves me with disdain and disgust or pity and feigned sympathy for anyone who has not been able to meet my standards or join my circle. This kind of comparison serves only to demean others and I ignore the revelations about myself. It is from the pit of Hell.

One of my favorite movies is *The Greatest Game Ever Played.* It is a true story of how Frances Ouimet, a twenty-year-old amateur won the 1913 US Open at The Country Club Golf Course where he used to caddie. At the time, golf was a gentlemen's game and caddies were considered a part of the lower class, the underprivileged. The movie portrays the country club members as very reluctant to even allow Ouimet to participate in the amateur tournament, and a British nobleman discarded Ouimet's challenge to the British champion simply because of his low class standing.

This false sense of privilege and superiority over others is not a disease that only the accomplished and the "winners" among us—the upper class, if you will—are susceptible to. It also affects the poor and less privileged. Whether the disrespect is displayed as scorn and derision or snobbery and contempt, it is the dark side of attempting to use comparison and competition as the means to validate my life and quench the thirst in my soul.

One does not have to look hard to see it displayed in the very wealthy, the very accomplished, and the very poor and seemingly unskilled. This sense of superiority and entitlement displays itself in many ugly and hateful methods, condemning any and all who hold a differing view or opinion, often at the same time demanding validation of their own views with an inability or unwillingness to see the fault in themselves.

They say we are a divided nation and the last three presidential elections seem to support that claim. It is not the differences that divide us. Derision and contempt has replaced the respect and honor that we owe each other as fellow human travelers with differing experiences and opinions. We want to be different from everyone, and yet there is a strong push to make everyone conform to our way of thinking and our ideals.

This is the path I must vigilantly guard myself against following. If I allow myself this path, I will never find the enjoyment of who I am, my gifts, and my life. All I can expect from a sense of superiority and snobbery is anger, contempt, and hatred.

The pleasure of God

You and I are more complicated than simply the sum of our differing gifts and talents, however few or many we may possess. Occasionally we might find some affirmation for using a gift or talent, but if I am to discover the self that I am and the life I dream of, it will not be found in the gift or the affirmation I hope to receive. The life I am looking for, the life I want to live simply cannot be squeezed out of the gifts and talents I've been given. They are meant for my enjoyment to use much like a new bicycle on my tenth birthday, but they do not have the power to birth the life I want. My gifts and talents are not me. I can improve them or lose them, but they are much like my bicycle, meant to get on and ride like the wind, and when I do I sometimes feel as if I'm flying.

Eric Liddle was a gifted runner. He was fast, very fast. He was the Scottish Olympic Gold medalist in the 400 meter event in the 1924 Olympics. Harold Abrams was fast as well. He also won a gold medal in the 1924 Olympics. The difference between the two runners was that Liddle enjoyed his gift, and running for him was a form of gratitude to God who had gifted him with speed. Abrams ran because he was compelled to win in an effort to prove himself, to prove his worth. He needed validation.

Abrams, as portrayed in the movie, *Chariots of Fire*, was unable to enjoy his gift of speed, and found little satisfaction in winning. Liddle, in contrast, enjoyed running as the gift it was. One of my favorite lines was when Liddle said to his sister, "When I run I feel His (God's) pleasure."

That seems like life to me, enjoying my gifts and discovering the pleasure of God.

As I travel this path, I would like to better know the gifts I have been given. If I never stand up to be compared, if I never measure myself against anyone else, I will never know I can sing, and I might spend my life in silence.

Comparison and competing can be useful, helping me to understand both what I can and cannot do. They help me discover my gifts. Eric Liddle would have never known he was fast if he had not run against another competitor.

The point in the comparison is not to find out how bad I am or someone else is. The point is not to humiliate the losers or those who don't have the same gifts. The point is the discovery of what gifts and talents I have and to enjoy them— and even to encourage and admire the talents of others to affirm their gifts. Simply because I have a gift or talent doesn't mean I must force it into public view, or that anyone else is obligated to enjoy it.

If I want to live and enjoy life I must use the gifts I have been given to use. To do otherwise would be to despise them.

In seventh grade I was afraid of the public laughter and humiliation I expected from attempting to sing my part. That day became significant after hearing Ms Ford's compliment. Laughter and humiliation would have been painful, but it would have been worse if she had been critical of my efforts, telling me I couldn't sing all that well in an effort to protect her own sense of achievement and worth.

I might have missed the enjoyment of music and the singing I have experienced over the years. I might have become even more of a "professional critic," not only cutting myself off from the ability to enjoy my gifts, but finding myself unable to enjoy the gifts of others. If someone had not helped me identify something I could do well, I might have been unable to enjoy Tiger's miracle putts or his phenomenal recovery shots. I might not have been able to enjoy the accomplishments of my friends or my brothers or to admire the talents of a competitor or the talents of my spouse.

I would only be concerned with me.

Failure is not the worst thing that can happen to me. Failure teaches me my limitations. It teaches me where I am not gifted or talented. It is important to know I do not have the talent to correctly change the brakes on my car or I am not qualified to perform brain surgery.

The worse thing that could happen is not that I might fail in my attempts to compete. The worse thing would be to use my gifts and talents in a effort to find life in the affirmation and recognition I want from them, and then in my disappointment from not being able to get enough, find I have either turned into a critic or a condescending snob, looking down on others, treating them with contempt and disrespect.

That's the worst thing that could happen to me.

And yet the arrogance and snobbery I disdain are two sins that threaten to keep me from the life I want—because I find those sins within me.

Six

It's All About Sin

God accepts me in my sin. My sin is all I really have to offer Him. I wish it weren't so, but I think sin is all that I really have to bring to Him except for possibly my pain and sorrow. My purity is not pure enough and my goodness is not good enough. In fact, they are filth in His eyes, but He opens His arms in delight and warmly accepts me when I humbly come to Him with my sin. My sin is all I have to offer Him.

It can't be all that bad, can it?

I know I am not immune to the problems of humanity. I have my share of problems, plenty of them. And I freely confess I would not rank at the top of the goodness scale if there were such a scale. It wouldn't be too difficult to find someone more generous, or more considerate, who would respond more kindly and behave better in many situations than I do. Comparatively speaking, I am not all that good when it comes to goodness.

Yet I am not all that bad either. Frankly I don't understand what the problem is within me that is so big and so ugly, so stiff and so broken that it required Jesus to come and suffer such a cruel and tortuous death on a cross? How could anything I have ever done demand such a gruesome punishment as payment or restitution?

Surely God could have dealt with my sin differently? Surely God could have dealt with my shortcomings without being so harsh.

Let me be clear, I'm not trying to minimize my failings or my recurring problems. I think I'm getting better at admitting my problems and my failures even when I don't want to. I don't claim to live up to even my own expectations, and I often find myself pretending these problems of mine, my failures, don't exist. I'm not trying to argue I am better than I really am. I've already admitted I wouldn't rank all that high on the goodness scale. I simply don't think I measure all that low on the scale either.

If I had known you twenty five-years ago, I would have told you I was not aware of any sin in my life. I didn't smoke, drink, or cuss, and I mostly did the things I knew I was supposed to do. I was faithful to my wife, I provided for my family, I was an active participant in a community of faith, and I helped others when an opportunity presented itself, at least most of the time. I made time for personal reflection, prayer, and study. At the time, to the best of my knowledge, there was nothing in my life I knew to be sinful.

In twenty-five years I have grown older and I believe a bit wiser. In this journey I have discovered things within me I simply couldn't see before, things that are not very attractive, and of which I am not very proud. Maybe I couldn't see them before because I didn't have the courage to face them.

I told you I was faithful to my wife and provided for my family.

I was.

And I did.

As I learned to listen to my wife and children I discovered they did not require me to be their personal drill sergeant instructing them on the correct and proper way to live, nor did they appreciate the effort. I thought that was what it meant for me to be their leader, to be the head of the house and the man of the family. Over time I could see in their responses to me, and sometimes I could hear in their voices what they needed in me was a leader to help them discover how to live a life of their own.

They needed an example, not an instructor.

What they really wanted was to hear my questions, to see my struggles and to share in my victories much more than the demonstration of only fulfilling my duties. They did want my guidance and wisdom. But most of all, they wanted to search with me and discover together what living is all about. They taught me leadership was not holding them to my expectations, standards even I couldn't live up to.

Maybe they were the ones who helped me gain the courage I needed to be more honest with myself. Maybe it was in that process where I began to discover a gentle strength I had not understood before. Perhaps it was as I began to listen to their hearts that I gained insight into my own and began to better understand the desires of my heart and learn more about my passion to live life as God meant it to be lived.

Twenty-five years ago I didn't know how to be that kind of leader. I only knew how to be stiff and angry, mistaking anger and hardness for the strength a man lives by. I didn't know how to be different, and I didn't know how to give them what they needed most from me. I didn't realize that, while I thought I had no sin, I was failing at what was most important to me, being a husband to my wife and a father to my children.

As I began to see my failures and be more honest with myself, I also became more aware of the sin I couldn't see within me. As I began to pay more attention to myself and listen to the dialogue inside my head that keeps me company throughout the activity of any given day, my thoughts would sometimes intrude into my conversations, as if to interrupt my sentences, distracting me from the topic. Many of these rambling thoughts were benign and innocent companions, while others were cancerous parasites I would feed, finding them at the same time to be both detestable and desirable. Often the voice of these unholy thoughts would embarrass me even though I was the only one to hear them; yet at the same time I often felt drawn to those thoughts, even when I knew them to be forbidden.

Even as I admit this, I am ashamed. I suspect there are times I blush for what might appear to be no reason at all. No reason except for what only I know to be true, what I know to be within me. Then there are the times when I should blush with embarrassment and don't.

In this process of coming to myself, I have also discovered times when I am resentful about helping another. Someone might be in true need, and all reason and logic argues I should be glad to participate and help for a number of very good reasons. Yet within me, for a reason beyond my comprehension I feel resentful, and I find it impossible to separate myself from the feelings and the barrage of internal complaints that seem to linger within me.

Not to make it sound like I am the victim. I am a willing participant. There are times when I simply behave badly.

"You're only human" is the comfort well-meaning friends have offered when they witness such a failure, as long as it is not one of the "big sins." I don't find much comfort in knowing my failures qualify me as part of the human gene pool, and that the rest of humanity shares in my inability to get life right. Excusing myself simply because no one else has got it right offers me very little comfort in my failures.

You already know I've applied a good deal of effort to get life right. In spite of my best attempts, no matter how hard I've tried, I simply have been unable to get it right. Over and over again I find my best efforts fall short of the goodness I think I should live, the goodness I want to live. I am so far from perfect. I am not even able to live up to my own expectations.

There have been times I have stumbled into, with no forethought or plan, a misdeed—one I had no intention of committing.

Sometimes.

But not all of my misdeeds are incidental.

There have also been times I find myself willingly doing the things I know to be wrong. At times I have chosen with intention and forethought to do what I know I shouldn't, planning and executing the very thing I am opposed to. I can offer an explanation for my incidental sin, excusing it as unintentional but what troubles me most is the intentional offense. It lingers like a bad smell, reminding me of my choice, and it is not so easily excused with an apology or a reason.

And so I confess, I am not all that good. What I was unable to see in my life twenty-five years ago I see much better now. Sometimes I wish I couldn't see it, but I cannot unsee what I now know. Regardless of my intent or purpose, this sin I now see is mine. It belongs to me. There is no one else to blame.

You may be able to better see my point now and agree with me when I disqualify myself in the test of goodness. But I will again argue that I am not all that bad. I am no serial killer. I am no drug dealer. I am not a thief, I don't gamble and I don't *dance!* In spite of my failures, there are plenty of good things I do! I give part of my income to the church and charities, even when I find myself resentful I try to help others when I can. I do work hard at being a good husband

and father. *Sometimes I even slow down and let a car pull out in front of me in traffic!*

I know I am not without fault. I am not trying to hold myself up to be a model of goodness for others to follow. I admit I fall short.

But have I fallen so far and come so short—are these transgressions of mine so great that they required such a high price that the innocent Jesus had to suffer such a cruel death because of these shortcomings?

How can my failures, common, and often harmful only to me; how can these misdeeds and this sin of mine demand such a high price? It seems the punishment does not fit the crime. It seems excessive.

And what exactly did Jesus' death do for me?

It didn't eliminate my sin, because as painful as it has been to admit, with a good deal of effort, I have just confessed I still sin. So what did His death accomplish for me?

If His death was meant to deal with my sin, why do I still sin?

And what am I supposed to do with this sin that still plaguing me like an incurable disease?

The problem of sin is much bigger than I imagined

What is very evident is that God believes sin is a big deal. This issue of sin is much more serious to Him than it is to me.

I don't believe I would have suffered so much to take care of the problem if I were in His position. God is pretty clear this issue of sin is the primary obstacle in my search to finding the life I want. It obstructs all progress; it impedes all of my effort to advance in the search to discover life.

Given the difficulty in attempting to manage such a greasy problem, it is not surprising to me that God would spend a good deal of time addressing this common dilemma of sin in the Bible. He even correlates sin with death, which might explain why God's response to it was sometimes rather harsh and downright unfriendly at times.

Just to clarify, death is not my goal. However there are fleeting moments when death attempts to seduce me into believing it might offer a release from the chaos and frustration of my futile efforts.

Death is not what I thirst for. It holds no answer to the search.

I am left with the conclusion that if I really want to discover the life I long for, I must better understand how I am to deal with this issue of sin, especially if sin is leading me to death.

I don't know much about Madeleine L'Engle, but from reading a few short paragraphs she has written, I do know she is a woman with incredible insight. She reasoned we are guaranteed to keep sinning in spite of our best efforts, because no matter how hard we try, we cannot eliminate the influence of sin in our lives, leaving us doomed to have our attempts at doing good stained by our flawed nature, as sin permeates every aspect of life.

That is discouraging.

It is discouraging to realize I am no more able to manage the sin in my life than I am able to manage my own thoughts. The good thoughts and bad alike are intermingled, intertwined, and inseparable as if joined together. I think about giving to someone and then think about how it will benefit me. Or I may slow down to let someone in traffic only to get angry when a second driver crowds in behind them. The thoughts have seemingly merged. Both good and bad form my thinking. When I try to form a plan the thinking only insures the thoughts continue—both the good and bad alike.

And so my effort to manage my bad thoughts only insures they persist. I can no more eliminate them than I can intentionally stop breathing or stop the blood from pulsing through my veins. Every effort only ensures it will continue to lurk within me. I am slowly becoming more aware of the insidious nature of this sin. I am beginning to understand it has subtly and with sinister intent, tangled itself within my very soul, and often disguises itself as me. I am unable to separate it from even my most noble good deeds, and I find it mingled and blended within everything I do.

What is left for me to do when all of my most valiant efforts fall far short of ridding me of the very thing that inhibits me from obtaining life, God-given and God-designed?

It seems this sin of mine is not such a small issue as I had first thought.

The fact that God is very serious about sin is an understatement. God went to great lengths to deal with sin and the effects it has had on this planet. He includes even the smallest of wrongdoings in His list of transgressions. I find there to be a corruption within me of which I have no control, and try as I might, I am simply unable and incompetent to lay hold of life as I desire to live it.

Even in my faith, I am left with nothing I can do. Once again, I am forced to look to God with my questions and my failures. Even when there is no other place to go and nothing left to do, I find a resistance within me to turn, a reluctance to look to the only One who has addressed this problem.

It seems that this is a much bigger problem than I ever imagined. What conspires within me and against me, what is it that presses me to work harder at my goodness, rather than turn to God who has demonstrated the power over this bent nature in me?

I am so intent on doing something and doing it myself. When will I learn I am far too small, and this problem far too great for my feeble abilities?

I spend all of my energy attempting to manage this evil within me, and all I seem to be able to do is feed it. All of my effort only guarantees this insidious sin of mine continues within me.

Sin urges me on, pushing me to do better, to try harder.

Then sin compliments me on my valiant efforts.

Finally, sin tells me I haven't tried nearly hard enough, all the while keeping me from turning and trusting the One that can and has provided the solution to it all.

Perhaps this is why my sin demanded such desperate measures? He knew it to be the only means to eradicate the hold it has on my soul.

Maybe I have been right all along? Maybe these offenses I commit are not all that significant? Maybe I have been looking only at the symptoms and not the real problem?

It seems these failures of mine are not the real issue, but merely a symptom of the malevolence that hides and breeds within me. I believe I am coming to understand my real transgression, the root of the issue within me. It is my that I refuse the help of the only One who can help me, the rescuer who holds out His hand, offering me the very life for which I long and search for.

It is impossible for me to judge the depth or magnitude of my sin merely by my transgressions. I must judge it by my persistent rejection of the only help that can overcome this sinister bent within me. The only help able to separate and disconnect it from me without destroying me in the process.

This sin that slips so easily out of my grasp, hiding so skillfully in the shadows of my soul, yet quickly manifests itself when threatened by my bowing before the Creator to request help. This sin of mine is never more visible than in my rejection of such eagerness to help me. Even in the face of my rejection He is willing to bleed for me, to bend down on

His knees and reach His hand out in a most compassionate offer to help me in my search.

He bends down low and I refuse to take His hand.

I turn away and increase my effort to do it myself, spurning His compassion.

No. My problem is not merely the transgressions of failing to be good. I can offer a more expanded list, but therein is not the problem. The problem is in the rejection of His love and my refusal of His generous offer to help me, trusting in my own abilities to solve the problem on my own.

The problem is I want to do it myself.

The shame engulfs me.

I am embarrassed at the exposure.

I know so little of love.

This independence I thought to be such strength to me, such a benefit and help, now pushes away the only pure and undefiled love I will ever know.

It's all about sin

Moses was chosen by God. Moses did not choose his path in life. He did not choose to be born an Israelite or to be raised by Pharaoh's daughter. He did not choose to be the one who led the Israelites from Egypt. He was one of the world's most famous men, appointed to a task that would write his name in history.

It was an assignment he didn't want.

Moses wasn't given many options. He did surrender to his assignment, and even then it was with a good deal of reluctance.

He led the Israelites on their first camping trip. They left homes and a routine they were familiar with in exchange for tents, little demands on their time, more stuff than they needed, and a newly found freedom. For the first time in their lives this generation of Israelites owned the responsibility for their own lives. They were now unemployed and no longer were under the commands of the foreman dictating their production schedules, criticizing their work, and cutting their lunch breaks short. They were now wanderers with no source of food or water.

They were free.

Along with their freedom came the privilege of responsibility.

When Moses left them alone for a few days the intoxication of the new found freedom quickly revealed their immaturity. Perhaps Moses didn't realize he had on his hands a million college students who found themselves in the sun and the sand. What do college students do in the sun and sand?

They call it *spring break*.

And the celebration turned corrupt quickly as they threw an unfettered party with no restraints but their own, and that was not enough.

Sunshine and sand with nothing to do and nowhere to go. Just waiting for Moses to come back off the mountain, but who really cares about Moses? Let's take off our clothes and party! And then they began to dance and bow before a golden calf, calling it their god.

God assigned Moses the task of leading the Israelites out of their life-numbing existence in Egypt. God provided for them. He gave them their freedom and He had plans of giving them their own property where they would have their own farms, where they could let their kids run and play, grow their own crops, and have their own livestock. But more than all the stuff, He was leading them to life; life they could only dream about before, but now this life was theirs with the only requirement being to follow His lead and trust Him as they went.

Rob Bell, in his book *Sex God*, helped me to learn the Ten Commandments God gave Moses and the Israelites were not simply a list of rules, directions on how to live. They were given as a love agreement, per their tradition. A love agreement that a husband makes with his new bride to outline the boundaries of the relationship. Both parties agree on the terms of their relationship and how it will work. These are the conditions of their love.

This was not a list from the drill sergeant. This was the list both the bride and groom agreed upon as the expression of their love for each other. The stones Moses brought down from the mountain were part of the wedding agreement between God and His treasured people, Israel. He called them His treasured possession.

The people agreed to follow this agreement. They approved of what God asked of them as their part of the relationship.

And they couldn't keep the agreement.

Later God called his people stubborn. He said they had a stubborn heart and would not listen to Him.[4]

God is a husband who loves His bride.

God knows better than to expect us to be able to achieve the high standards He sets. In fact, Jesus spent a good deal of His time teaching those who thought they had reached the standard, that the standard was higher than they thought. You may remember they were not happy with Him telling them they were not a good as they thought.

Following God is all about sin. It is the sin that tries to convince me I need no assistance and can find my way by myself. It is sin that seduces me into believing I can find life somewhere else other than with God. Sin persuades me that life is in the golden calf. Sin persuades me that God is a drill sergeant who is only interested in mindless obedience.

Finding life is the ambition, but the journey to life is all about sin.

Growing up, I attended many church services. Somehow along the way, I came to the conclusion the Bible was all about teaching people how to be good. I now think the Bible is more about helping me recognize I am not much different than the Pharisees in pretending I have risen above sin. The Bible is to help me realize how ineffective my methods at curing myself are, and that goodness is well out of my reach.

It is so much easier to identify the faults in someone else than it is to see my own. I am incredibly perceptive when it comes to recognizing the failures of others. But when it comes to *my* failures, they seem reasonable and not all that significant if they are even noticeable to me.

And when someone has the audacity to point out *my* failure, I have a hundred reasons and a thousand excuses. I find like Adam in the garden, my response is to hide myself and then deny and blame others for my sin. "The woman you gave me, she ..."

It's not my fault. If you hadn't given me ... if they had done it right ... I was minding my own business ...

I am a victim.

I am not responsible.

It's not my fault.

Like the Israelites, I am a freed slave. There is great responsibility given to us with freedom. I am responsible for my actions. I am responsible for my decisions. I am responsible for my choices.

Responsibility is the path to find life, and I am responsible for my sin. God paid a great price to deal with my sin; a lovely and innocent life. God knew that I would be thirsty. He knew I would be looking to find life, and He knew that the only way I would be able to find the life I wanted and for which I was made would be for Him to take sin to task.

Himself.

For me.

He is the Champion of my soul, as I have no power of my own to slay the dragon within. After all He has done for me it shouldn't be so, but often I am still reluctant to go to Him.

I am still reluctant to admit my failures. I am still reluctant to go to Him with dirt on my hands and face. I want to clean up before I approach Him. I want to be presentable.

Yet all that He requires of me is to be honest about my sin and to go to Him. There is where He meets me, with honest admission of my failure. It is there in my sin that the knowing and loving God has promised to breathe life into this soul of mine.

It is the relationship I've been looking for all my life.

Seven

In the Image

"God only knows what I'd be without you"
—The Beach Boys

Wilderness flowers

A friend and I decided to get away for the weekend and go on what for me was a long overdue backpacking trip into the mountains. I was living in San Jose at the time, and we went to the California coast to hike into Big Sur State Park. With our provisions for the weekend stuffed into the packs, we embarked on what was to be a fifteen mile hike into the wilderness—fifteen miles in both directions. I had grown up camping and hiking in the Cascade Mountains in Washington State and was looking forward to being in the woods again. It had been three years since I had left my home in Washington State and at least that many years since I had a pack on my back and a trail to follow into the unknown.

My friend Dennis set a good pace as we left the trail head. I had the impression he was wrestling with life or running from it and had chosen to use the time and the woods to ponder his confusion without looking it the eye. Having a four or five inch height advantage over me and most of him legs, he was able to cover more ground than I could, stride for stride. For the first five miles or so I was able to pace him in spite of his advantage. After the first five miles the extra effort began to take its toll on me, and Dennis began to put some distance between us on the uphill climbs. Soon he had put enough distance between us that he was out of sight.

Alone with my thoughts, the woods, and the trail, I walked at my own pace, enjoying the outdoors and the unfamiliar plant life. One flowering plant native to the area caught my attention as particularly glorious. It seemed to reach toward the sky with a large bushy flower atop of a two or three foot stem. It was a really cool flower that seemed quite at home in the coastal climate of California. The beauty of the display was accentuated by the flower's isolation, as the plants seemed to be scattered about the wilderness floor, one here, two over there, and on they went.

As I hiked, enjoying and considering these unique floral displays, it occurred to me that of all the population, only a few would ever hike this trail, and fewer still would venture this far into the woods where they might have the opportunity to enjoy the display I was seeing. By the looks of the plants and considering the dryer climate than what I was used to in the Cascades, I had the impression the flowers I was looking at might only bloom for a few days a year, and by chance I had stumbled into those few days to witness the beauty of the flowering plants visible from my forest walkway.

They received no attention and no care out here in this wilderness. They simply grew without regard for the occasional hiker like me who would happen to wander by.

As I walked and looked, I thought about the flowers alongside the trail and those that were just out of sight. Then I thought about the ones that might be on the other side of the hill and still others that would never be seen from the path, out of view, never to be seen, never witnessed or enjoyed by anyone. It seemed sad to me, almost wasteful that such beauty went unnoticed, offering no benefit, growing, flowering, and dying in their isolation.

"That's a waste." I thought to myself.

"Why would you grow these flowers out here in the woods where no one will ever see them and no one will ever enjoy them? What good are they?"

"They serve the purpose for which I created them and when they do that they glorify Me."

There was no booming voice and there were no burning bushes. Yet the voice was as clear to me as if the words were spoken out loud. (And I learned later these flowers are appropriately known as Our Lord's Candle.)

My perspective of the flowers that were scattered throughout the woods, especially those which I would never see, suddenly took on a greater significance for me then what I had held for them a moment ago. With hesitation in my gaze I glanced from flower to flower as the trail led me past them. I had become an intruder. This was their domain, and I felt I was interfering in their worship. I had assumed these flowers were here for me to enjoy. Now I believed the flowers that no one would ever see might have intentionally moved away from the trail, out of sight to a place where they could worship God without interruption. The forest in which I walked had been transformed into a sanctuary, and I was being allowed to witness the anthem of gratitude as each plant stood tall, reaching toward heaven in praise of their creator, fulfilling the intent of their existence.

I once heard someone say that we humans are the only species on the planet that spend our time wishing we were somehow different, wishing we were someone or something else. Not only do we spend time thinking about it, but we spend a good deal of money and considerable effort attempting to change who we are, or at least the way others perceive us.

I am no exception.

As I search and travel this path to discover life, I have made many and various attempts to resolve the constant tension that seems to have burrowed itself within my soul. It has made a comfortable home in me. I don't know how this tension was birthed, and it seems that if I could only be different or better or smarter the tension would leave, along with its companions, uncertainty and insecurity. If only I could be different. And so I make every attempt to change, using anything that might offer an end to the chaos, so that I might discover who and what I was meant to be.

Maybe if I can find the place I belong and know my purpose I'll discover what I am looking for.

I wish I could be as content as those flowers that simply grow and stretch themselves heavenward. I wish I could fulfill my purpose as easily as they do, just by being.

Since my hike I discovered a quote by St. Irenaeus, "The glory of God is man fully alive."

That is what I want—to be fully alive.

Why do I have such dissatisfaction with myself? Where does it come from? What does it look like to live life "fully alive?"

How do I find my place in the created order, the place made for just me?

Do I have to be noticed by someone else to find that place? Would it matter to me if anyone noticed me or not? Do I have to be important or does it matter if my life is to be lived in insignificance, leaving little or no mark after I pass? If I am able to leave a mark for others, do I have the courage to put my name to it?

We really do need each other

I was channel surfing one night, and oddly enough I stumbled across a program that caught my attention. As I watched it began to provide some insight and a few answers to my questions about being human and living life.

The program I discovered was on the Learning Channel, and the topic that had caught my interest was *feral children*. It caught my attention because these children had been literally abandoned to live with animals or locked for years in a room with no human interaction. These were the children of fables I had grown up with, such as Tarzan or Mowgli, some living with wolves or dogs as their families. That was where the similarity ended. These children had been left with little or no ability to relate with people. There seemed to be little hope they would ever be able to find a life of closeness or even casual friendships with other humans.

The program had found several severe cases of abandoned or abused children. They were documenting a child's ability to learn words and communication skills after having been rescued and introduced into a healthy family environment. It was discouraging to watch as these children did not have the capacity to learn the language skills that life requires—learning that comes naturally for most of us as we interact with others. It was so evident that when a child is denied basic human interaction as a natural ingredient of growing, learning, and discovering with family and friends, the child is deprived of the ability to relate and function as humans were intended.

I am well aware much of television programming is presented with a point of view that often ignores the facts of the situation, and documentaries are sometimes the worst offenders. Regardless of the point of view being presented, it was clear that as a result of abuse and neglect by those who would normally have nurtured them, these children had suffered permanent damage.

I do not know what led the children's parents to make the choices they made. I will never know. I do not excuse them. I do not condone them. And I resist the urge to quickly condemn them since I simply do not know.

What I do know is that relationship is essential to our humanity. Children desperately need parents. Husbands need wives and wives need husbands.

We need family, friend, allies, and champions.

Left to myself, I am a feral child, incapable of becoming what I was created to be.

Relationship is a vital element of my search to discover life.

This program on feral children demonstrated to me a truth evident to most of us; family plays a crucial role in our development and preparation for living life. Relationships are first formed and modeled in the circumstance and framework of family. Regardless of the popular drivel to the contrary, the created design is that each of us develop and grow into the person we were created to be in and through the nurture and care of relationship, most particularly the relationship in the circumstance and framework of family.

I do understand there are situations that have prevented the father and mother from fulfilling the ideal family situation, such as death or long absences required by occupation or other circumstances. I know there are noble and courageous single parents who have nurtured children well in the face of great challenges. There are parents who have adopted to give children what their biological parents were unable to or chose not to provide. These single parents and the parents who chose to give up their children for adoption, believing that they couldn't fulfill the needs of a child, deserve appreciation for their efforts to provide the human intimacy and experience of relationship that a child needs.

I also understand and am fully aware there are those family conditions filled with abuse and violation of the person, thieving from children and wreaking havoc on the child's life instead of offering the caring provision they ought to have and deserve. These all-too-common situations are damaging as well, leaving their evil marks on the souls of children who must bear the scars for years to come.

But even in the distortion of what should be, there is in the heart of each of us that which could be—the craving to be loved and cared for and the longing for relationship.

I am created to live in relationship. Even when I suffer abuse, I still long for relationship.

It is in the very fiber and soul of who I am, of who we are.

We learn and live and grow in family, with people.

As we grow and mature, we venture into the world to interact with and learn from each other. We find friendship and help and love from each other. Loving ourselves just isn't enough.

The most satisfying events in my life have been when I can share an experience with someone I enjoy. My accomplishments are much more meaningful when there is someone who is interested in hearing about them and what they mean to me.

Have you ever tried to celebrate alone?

Throw a party by yourself?

I think you get the picture.

I'm not saying these relationships are easy or all blissful. G.K. Chesterton underscores the problem when he said, "The family is ... like a little kingdom, and, like most other little kingdoms, is generally in a state of something resembling anarchy."

Personally, I hate anarchy. It messes up my attempts to order and arrange my life.

I really wish it were easier.

It is by definition, chaos and confusion. There is enough confusion and chaos in my life already. My family is no exception to Chesterton's observation. We resemble that; anarchy and confusion, rarely finding a harmonious moment.

It is perplexing to me and only adds to the tension I feel. I find myself pulled between my acknowledged need for relationship and my effort to separate myself from the chaos and confusion of life. I need relationship, yet that is also where I have suffered the most disappointment and damage, in and from the relationship with the people I care the most about.

I find myself dealing with this tension by being very careful about what and how much I reveal about myself, and to whom I reveal it. I find I am always looking for cover, protection from anyone who might cause me harm or humiliation. I know I am not the only one with this dilemma of relationship. We spend a good deal of time and money searching for it, singing about it, or reading about it. We all seem to know how important it is and we pay to hear about how it could be, to be reminded that we've lost it and that we are still looking for it.

I have witnessed people who came to the hospital emergency room to simply sit in the presence of other people as a means to relieve their loneliness. The emergency room provided a sense of relationship for them. I can think of a thousand other places I would rather sit or search than in a hospital emergency waiting room.

For some, the search is for a sexual liaison offering them a taste of the relationship they want without much of the chaos. There is an ever-growing community of on-line personalities who search to fulfill their needs in the privacy of the public internet. We are a people in constant search, using any method that seems to promise what we long for and think we need.

Wherever the search might take us, much of life is spent pursuing the relationship we are desperate to find. Seldom will we hear it said out loud, but we are painfully aware of our search and our need to find relationship—and finding it or not means finding life or not.

What other reason would compel us to spend so much time, money, and effort on the search?

I became aware of my search as I became aware of my desire to find a soul mate, one who would journey and struggle alongside me. It also presented the most confusion to me and the greatest risk. I became acutely aware of this desire during my years in junior high school.

Perfect timing for me! (And probably most of my classmates as well.) It caught me at the peak of my insecurity and social ineptitude. I couldn't fully comprehend what was beginning for me. I simply wondered if there might be a young woman who would find me interesting, who might want to join souls and journey together. Perhaps what made life so confusing was that I was still learning and discovering me. How could I know someone else fully before I knew myself?

I made a few attempts and suffered as many failures. I learned to hide in the crowd as a way to protect myself from the humiliation I felt in my failed attempts. Hiding may not seem to be the most effective method to search for a soul mate. However ineffective it may be, it does offer a sense of safety that is hard to argue with.

My technique was to keep a low enough profile so as to go unnoticed, not risking too much exposure that all too often would end up as public ridicule. I would only venture into situations offering the possibility of a somewhat friendly reception. It was my hope in the process I would find an attractive young lady that might like me.

Music offered a place to play this game of hide and seek. The safety in listening to music is that the exposure was limited. All I needed was a melody with a good beat and as much volume as I could afford, and there were others that enjoyed the same music as I did. My only exposure was my personal taste in music, and it wasn't all that risky.

The music also offered a common bond of friendship with others who shared my interest. We shared new songs, new bands, and the experience of concerts. It became my community of friends as we each engaged in our personal search to find out about life. Music was our common interest.

I even recall some concerts where the music wasn't very good, at least in my opinion. Yet I still remember talking afterwards about the concert with my friends about how cool we thought the concert was and how much we all enjoyed it. Looking back I suppose I was agreeing with the popular opinion again to protect myself. I didn't want to lose my community of friends and was afraid if I said I thought the band stunk, I would risk losing my friends. Even if the music wasn't that great, I enjoyed the experience being with them. The friendship was what mattered most to me.

I didn't find my soul mate during that time. I was learning about me, my life, who I was, and what I should be about. The friends I made during that time are ones I can still visit many years later. The bond of those years still exists, even though we have traveled very different paths to where we are today.

The program on feral children may not have taught me anything really new. It did affirm for me what had been part of my life for years—that a vital part of being alive and being human is to be found in and through relationship. If relationship is stripped from my human experience, I will be left crippled and unable to fully experience life as it is meant to be lived.

It reminded me of my hike and what I learned in the Big Sur wilderness—that I will be most satisfied when I learn to be what I am created to be—just like the flowers that stood tall reaching toward the heavens as they grew in their random locations on the forest floor.

They were created to be flowers. I was created to be human.

I was created to live in relationship.

Created for relationship

It was God who said, "It is not good for man to be alone."

I didn't say that. It is the way He made things. As I have searched to discover life and how to live life as it was intended for us to live, I've taken my question to many places. I've read the Genesis creation account many times but didn't see much there that looked like it could help me.

Years after my junior high days and my hike in Big Sur, while reading about marriage, I began to look again at what had always been a curious sentence to me. In the Genesis account God says as He is creating man, "Let Us make man in our image."

It always kind of puzzled me, because God goes to great lengths to emphasize to His people that He is our one God, and that there are not many gods—yet here He says "Us."

Us is a plural. It means at least two, not one. When someone refers to themselves as "us" I am left wondering if they are all there.

I didn't press it all that hard years ago. There are many things I simply do not understand. I had been taught about the Trinity and chalked the sentence up to the "us" being relevant to the Trinity and creation, but it was still curious to me.

I mean, how can God be both "One" and an "Us" at the same time?

There have been many attempts to explain the concept of the Trinity, and they are useful in some ways, but I don't know how to comprehend a person that is three persons and one at the same time. It is far more difficult to me than calculus or quantum physics; I just don't understand.

What I am beginning to understand is that this relationship within the Trinity is very, very close. They are so close in relationship that the person of God would be fragmented if it were possible to separate the "Us." God is so tightly integrated we cannot explain Him by using three candles with three flames, or water, ice, and steam.

God is completely other, completely holy, and so intense in relationship, that relationship is an essential and basic part of who He is.

And then He said, "Let Us make man (*and woman*) in Our image."

As I began to admit my own desire and need for relationship, I better understood what God meant in the sentence in the creation account. Human-kind was created after the likeness of the God who exists in relationship. A relationship so close that when Philip asked Jesus to show him the Father, Jesus told Philip that when Philip had seen Jesus, he had also seen the Father. It is a relationship so intimate that Jesus said when the Spirit would make His home in us, the Father and Jesus would be there as well, making their homes in us.

We are created to be in relationship just as God lives in relationship. "In Our own image," He said. We are created in that image. I have been created to live in and for relationship. It is a part of my DNA, a part of my soul.

We really do need each other.

I spend so much time hiding and looking in all the wrong places for relationship. The need for relationship is part of my design. Looking is not all wrong. God created me to have relationship with more than only Him. But if I miss Him, I miss it all.

If I miss Him, how can I, in my need, offer relationship to someone else that has the same design, the same need within them? It seems to me we will both be asking something of the other, asking for something neither of us possess. How can I give you something I don't have?

If I can't find satisfaction in relationship without God, then I how do I find Him? If He is the One who made me, and He made me for Himself, how do I discover Him? He is beyond my understanding.

And He seems to only show up when He wants to, and then not all that often.

How can I hope to know Him unless He chooses to reveal Himself in a way that I can understand Him? If I can't understand at least a little of Him, I haven't much hope of knowing Him, and even less hope for a relationship with Him.

God is not predictable. As CS Lewis wrote, "He is not tame." I cannot demand Him to show up or manipulate Him to reveal Himself. I am literally on a hike through life, waiting for Him to interrupt me, when, where, and however He pleases. He chooses His time on the path, and I often feel very thirsty, waiting and hoping He might show up for the need that He created in me.

The interesting part of this need I have for relationship with God is that He has the same desire to know me as I have to know Him. He is drawn to me and you just as we are drawn to Him.

Really?

He wants to know me too?

For me it was demonstrated unexpectedly, when He interrupted my ponderings on a hike in the Big Sur wilderness. It was a small voice, speaking to me. What He said about the flowers was important, but more important to me was that He was speaking to me. It was the Father's voice to a child wandering, searching with more questions than I could put words to. It was a moment when I felt His compassion and His care. He spoke to me in a way I could understand.

I expect He speaks often to me, but I don't hear Him. This time I heard, and I hold on to that memory. It is a memory that helps me understand who I am, what I am made for, and that I am loved.

Sometimes I forget. Sometimes my doubts and fears and busy nothings crowd out the memory of that moment, that time. It is a battle to remember, especially when my feelings contradict the memory.

I forget so easily. I want to live life fully human, in the relationship as He made me. But I am still so very thirsty. I want more life, and I find I don't easily give up my hide-and-seek tactics. I fall so easily into looking in all the wrong places when God seems to be so quiet and as hard as I try...

... I can't hear His voice.

Eight

Thou Shalt Have No Other God

We're all looking for love and meaning in our lives
We follow the roads that lead us
To drugs or Jesus —Tim McGraw, Drugs or Jesus

Ten thousand years and still going

I grew up in a small community church. It was a tall single story building with a steep pitched roof and old, weathered siding. The bats had found a way to get up and in-between the siding, inside the wall, and would nest there during the day. You could often hear them squeaking during the pastor's message on Sunday mornings. The church had hand-me-down wooden pews, well-used by the previous owners, and one or two were cracked. If you weren't careful you would be pinched when you would sit down in them.

The routine of the Sunday morning service always began by singing three or four hymns mixed with the announcements and offering, followed by the sermon. It always ended with the singing of one final hymn. I remember singing "Amazing Grace" as a young boy, restlessly standing on the wood floor, half gazing out the window, anxious to have the two hours at church completed so we could go home, or outside, or anywhere else where I would not have to be still and listen. "Amazing Grace" was one of the favorites in the mix of musical selections for Sunday mornings. I remember on one Sunday we sang, "When we've been there ten thousand years bright shining as the sun, we've no less days to sing God's praise, then when we first begun" while looking out the window at the trees and considering what it would be like to sing for ten thousand years.

Frankly, singing for ten thousand years was more frightening to me than it was comforting. Standing on the wood floor, singing for twenty minutes was almost unbearable, and since the weekly routine was to sing the songs while standing up with books in hand, I imagined standing in a crowd of thousands and thousands of people, all standing, and all singing.

It made my feet hurt to think of standing for ten thousand years. I couldn't stand still for ten minutes, and I could not imagine standing and singing for years and years and years.

How am I going to stand still for ten thousand years?

I suppose it could be attributed to the wandering mind of a young boy, but the images of God and heaven that formed in my mind during the many services I sat in were not very attractive to me. They said heaven was a good place. In my mind that meant the bad place must be really, really bad, if standing and singing for ten thousand years was what I had to look forward to in the good place.

One of the other points emphasized in my developing mind was that someday, and no one knew when, Jesus was going to come back to take everyone who believed in Him to heaven, leaving the ones who did not believe behind to suffer in the tribulation before they went to hell. This point definitely left an impression.

I still can't say I understand what it all means, but I knew then as well as now, none of it sounds very pleasant. Even then, when considering ten thousand years of singing (and it felt more like punishment than reward), I knew without a great deal of thought, I did not want what was behind the tribulation door.

I knew where I wanted to end up and which door I wanted to walk through. What really troubled me was the uncertainty of my final destination. It seemed there was so much that had to be done proper and right and I simply was not sure if I would make the cut when Jesus came back. I suspect all of this resulted in what might be today called a low grade of separation anxiety, always a bit nervous the big event might have happened whenever I found myself alone.

I can remember one occasion when my mom took me shopping for clothes. Now if you had given me a choice of standing and singing in church or going clothes shopping with Mom, it would have been a difficult decision. I found both to be pretty boring, but at least while shopping with Mom I could wander around.

This time after a few minutes of drifting about searching for something worthy of my interest I looked up to discover

Mom was nowhere in sight. She was gone. My first reaction was panic. After looking around with urgency, searching from one rack of women's clothing to the other, I concluded Jesus had come, taken my mother, and I had been left behind to face the dreaded tribulation in the women's clothing department.

It simply couldn't get any worse than this!

I would be lying to you if I said this was the only time this had happened. There were other times as well. I would search, and eventually Mom would come out of the dressing room or from around the corner, and I would know I had been granted a reprieve and would not have to face the coming judgment in women's clothing.

This whole idea of the tribulation was very troublesome to me. It wore on me until one Sunday I heard the preacher say no one knows the day or the time when this big event would happen. This intrigued me. I thought about it, and as I thought about it I began to reason if no one knew the day or time when Jesus would return then Jesus couldn't return if someone "knew" when He was going to return.

I further reasoned if I thought Jesus was going to return "that year," then He couldn't, because I would have known about it!

Certainly there were many holes in my logic, but these were desperate times for me. So I looked up to heaven and said with as much confidence as I could muster, "I think you are coming back this year!"

I said it a couple of times to convince God I really "knew" it, and left it at that. I believed it would give me a year without the worry of being left behind to endure the tribulation. That left me with a year to see if I could figure it all out. I knew my reasoning wasn't air-tight, and there was a big risk of some serious miscalculations on my part, but it was the best and only plan I could come up with at the time.

It did offer me some comfort as I set my sights on the year ahead, leaving the worry about eternity for next year. As time passed and as I learned more, I also became more and more aware of my desire to find something more satisfying in life. On the way I gained a bit of confidence in my fate and destination as I learned more about God and life. Concurrently I grew less and less concerned about being left out. Singing for ten thousand years might be tolerable (although standing still for that long still concerns me!).

Growing up, I did learn one of the sure ways to fail at reaching heaven was to give in to a really bad thing called idolatry. Idolatry would definitely take me down the wrong path. So I had a keen interest to learn about idolatry and what it was.

In time, I learned idolatry was the misguided efforts of trying to find life apart from God. I was making progress in my attempt to figure things out and avoid the tribulation, so I applied myself to learning more about idolatry, what it meant, and how I could avoid it. I wanted to avoid falling into that trap. I was pretty excited when I learned a missionary was going to visit our Sunday School class on furlough from Africa with one of these dreaded "idols." This was my opportunity to see an idol up close and learn from someone who has had experience with idols. I would be able to know firsthand what they looked like and what I needed to do to avoid them.

This one was a stone idol and was shaped like a long face. The missionary told us it was a family idol and had been given to the missionary by one of the tribal leaders he had visited in Africa. I never understood why a missionary would bring one of these accursed idols back to church, when idols were one of the great offenses to God. I wasn't going to question it all, as I was committed to making the most of this opportunity to learn, in order to avoid the mistake the pagans make in bowing down to these idols.

The knowledge I gained from the experience offered me some welcome relief. It was interesting, because I found myself wondering why anyone would worship what was obviously a rock. I was relieved, because there was no danger of me bowing before a dumb rock in an attempt to find any help, let alone life.

I was in no danger of offending God with idol worship.

This was my reasoning, and as you already know, my reasoning is sometimes flawed and unsound. These early images of God were scary and not all that inviting. As the years passed and I became more aware of my thirst to find life, God was not the first place I turned in search of a drink.

To be honest with you, I'm not always sure how to go to God.

I can't tell you what going to God looks like, although many times I've been advised to go to Him. I can tell you as I have gotten older, I've come to know all idols are not faces made from rocks. I know this because I have bowed down to many other false gods in an attempt to squeeze a drink of life from them. After they would leave me thirsty and emptier than before I met them, I would leave that idol in search of another.

Caller ID

I wish God used caller ID, so I would know when He was talking to me.

And life would be much easier if all idols were made from rocks.

I am so thirsty for life. It is a constant ache in my soul, an increasing desire and a constant companion, this thirst. All of my attempts to smother it or eliminate it have been useless. I am thirsty to know life as I have been created to live it, relating to Him and to others. This "relationship," which is such an integral part of being human, in all of its confusion and all of the chaos is simply a hard place to live, and sometimes it all feels more like death to me than life.

I am so confused.

I try to hear His voice. I try to live in the relationship that He said He wants to have with me. I try to follow Him and most often end up messing it up in some way or another. There are so many voices claiming to know "God" and what He is saying, what He expects from me and how I am supposed to live before Him. Frankly, I've found it a very difficult task, attempting to know God and follow God without falling into the empty routine of religious activity that in the end seems to be self indulgent, serving only my interests.

You might be thinking here that if I want to hear God I should simply read my Bible. That's a great idea; God does speak to us through the Bible. There is simply too much evidence that it was assembled and orchestrated by someone who stands outside of time. It is such an amazing story to see how it has unfolded and is unfolding and He continues to speak and show Himself in the pages of the record.

However, knowing He speaks in and through the Bible, and hearing Him speak to me is not the same.

Many times I find the words simply stare back at me and seem to offer no message, no insight, and no voice. I do admit there are times when the words have seemed to leap off the pages and hurl themselves deep into my soul. I love those times, but they are not what I experience each time I sit down to read.

I often find myself straining to hear His voice.

Sometimes following the path seems effortless and doors I was never aware of swing wide open, leading me to places beyond my imagination. Other times I hear nothing. I strain to listen to the heart that God put within me, the heart that

He has breathed to life. Yet sometimes it seems He is the One who stands in my way, thwarting the path to realize the dream or the purpose I know He has given me.

I don't hear His voice.

I feel lost in my search.

I am overwhelmed with disappointment and confusion.

There is so much pain and discouragement in life and often God seems silent and careless in the midst of it all.

Then I wish all false gods were made of rocks. Perhaps I wouldn't find myself bowing to them so easily.

In my generation, we commonly bowed to drugs, sex, and Rock-n-Roll. These were not the only idols we bowed to; they were only the most popular. And we knew what we wanted from them as well.

In 1972 Dobie Gray released the song "Drift Away" written by Mentor Williams. I still enjoy hearing it. I find it to be a haunting melody with lyrics that speak to my life, my confusion, and the unquenchable desire to find some relief from all my turmoil. The song invites me to find freedom and joy by getting lost in the Rock-n-Roll and to simply "drift away."

I search in earnest for that place, a place to "drift away." A place where I can find the freedom from the chaos and confusion and taste the life I want so much to find. It is a God given desire, this longing to find freedom and life. But the trouble with using music to find what I need is it turns the music into a false god that I find myself bowing down to in a futile attempt to gain something music simply can't give me; life.

The same is true when I turn to sex or drugs or anything else I might use in an attempt to satisfy my deep desires for life. What I found as I bowed before each of these false gods was I was only wearing out my knees and trying to find what can't be found or given from any rock or idol.

I suppose that is what makes them idols, their impotence to meet my need for life.

I know the rocks are impotent but the difficulty is He has given me gifts to enjoy, gifts that lift me out of the dreary and into the pleasure of life. It is uncanny how I can take a gift and convert it into an idol, making it my false god. I bow before it demanding it give me life and once again I find the counterfeit cannot give me what I demand.

Sex is a glorious gift. It is a celebration of relationship that mimics the oneness found in God Himself. But it is not life. When I attempt to extract life from sex, demanding it give me what it cannot, it becomes distorted and disfigured into something it was never meant to be. And the more I try to extract life from it the more distorted and less satisfying it becomes.

The beauty and glory of sex fades into effort and performance under the weight of my demand it give me life.

When it becomes apparent life cannot be had from one idol, it is not difficult to find another hocking its promises of a better life. Drugs were a fashionable idol and offered to sedate my desire for life, a way to not feel the disappointment of my failure to find life. They were so popular a poster was published citing Genesis 1:29 where God declares He has provided us with all seed bearing herbs and trees for food, and that it was good. Once again a good gift misused, and like many idols, it seduces us into believing it can provide what only God can give. Then it leaves us with a craving for more, until the demands of the false god become our life, and we are rewarded with only the bondage of addiction.

There are numerous stories of people who have become so committed to finding life in their false god it destroys them, literally draining the life out of them and sending them to their grave. Maybe that is why God is so hateful of idols. They tempt us with an offer of life and then suck the life out of us, destroying us and others in the progression toward death, never living up to the promise of finding life, of living free and with joy.

Whether it is merely the comfort they offer or the empty promise of life, there are many substitutes that doggedly taunt me, offering an easy solution to my search. Many of them appear benign, even innocent, such as television or food. You can add to the list work and hobbies, even church and relationship, the list is endless. It would be so much easier if they were all rocks.

No wonder there are times when God seems to oppose my reach.

It is so easy for me to reach for the wrong things.

But I still find myself driven to find life. I need life, even if it kills me.

The great commandment

As I read through history as recorded in the Bible, I find God has put a good deal of effort into helping us find our way and discover the life He promised us. I blush as I am discovered bowing before these rocks that never fulfill me and only lead me to my own destruction. No one has given more or sacrificed so much that we might drink deeply and find life. Not a drink of stale and stagnant water, but a living water that births life richly, fully, and abundantly.

He has given so much of Himself to restore the relationship we lost when we turned from Him to find life on our own. He has gone to great lengths to give us all we need for life. He paid a high ransom. He gave us Himself in the life of His Son.

Recently there have been programs documenting real life circumstances that have resulted in a near death experiences. Many should have resulted in death but for the aid of a rescuer, a stranger who happened by or a responder to the 911 call for help. These stories are recreated with drama added for television viewing, and at the end of the program the rescued and the rescuer are united, often for the first time. Most of the stories portray a friendship formed out of sincere gratitude—gratitude expressed to the rescuer for the selfless action that saved a life.

Sitting on my couch and watching the scene and observing the faces of the two parties, I am moved, witnessing the gratitude that is not an uncommon expression on the face of the rescued. It is a gratitude going beyond words; there are no words able to convey the thankfulness they feel to the one who came to their rescue. As I watch the face of the rescuer, it seems he understands it as well, and is grateful in turn that he was there to offer the help required.

I have also heard stories of those rescued from a similar tragic situation who respond with anger and resentment for the injuries they suffered from the accident. It seems they respond with blame and anger to the one who saved them from death. (I suspect these are not very popular stories to be retold.) Some of them file claims against the one who saved them from death, as if they were responsible for the injuries sustained in the accident. Apparently they would rather be dead.

Enduring a debilitating injury would be very difficult. I cannot say how I would respond, having never endured such an event. Even so, I am quick to criticize the ingratitude of anyone who responds with anger to the person who saved her life. I simply believe it to be wrong.

Then I find myself guilty of the same ingratitude as well. Rescued from certain death, a generous offer of life extended to me, and I spurn the help and look to do it on my own. Hell bent in my self-destructive search to find life, Jesus comes to me saying, "I am the life." He freely offers me the very thing for which I long and work so hard to find on my own.

Then I hear Him say, *"Apart from Me you can do nothing."*[5]

"What does that mean?"

"Exactly what it says, you can do nothing apart from Me."

And then He says, *"Come to Me all you who are tired."*[6]

How do you suppose God feels after coming to rescue us, giving Himself for us, taking my sentence on Himself to save me from death? How do you suppose He feels when I look someplace else for what He knows only He can give me? How does He feel when I bow before my idols, asking them for life, when He knows that in the end, it will destroy me and destroy the good that He has created? How does He feel when He holds out His hands, offering me what I desperately want, yet I refuse to receive it from Him?

That must be why God is a jealous God, because He holds the answer to my search, to the desire of my heart and refuses to stand by while I try to find life from a false god, a substitute that in the end will kill me.

Perhaps my greatest sin is committed when I do not respond to Him with gratitude for rescuing me from death, and instead I complain and curse Him for what I don't have.

Jesus was asked, "Which is the greatest commandment?"

His reply should be no surprise, *"Love the Lord your God with all your heart and with all your soul and with all your mind. This is the first and greatest commandment."* [7]

Nine

The Story of Life

"And we shouldn't be here at all, if we'd known more about it before we started. But I suppose it's often that way. The brave things in the old tales and songs, Mr. Frodo: adventures, as I used to call them. I used to think that they were things the wonderful folk of the stories went out and looked for, because they wanted them, because they were exciting and life was a bit dull, a kind of sport, as you might say. But that's not the way of it with the tales that really mattered, or the ones that stay in the mind. Folk seem to have been just landed in them, usually—their paths were laid that way, as you put it. But I expect they had lots of chances, like us, of turning back, only they didn't. And if they had, we shouldn't know, because they'd have been forgotten. We hear about those as just went on—and not all to a good end, mind you; at least not to what folk inside a story and not outside it call a good end. You know, coming home and finding things all right, though not quite the same." —
Samwise Gamgee, *Lord of the Rings*, Tolkien

Rising above the chaos

I find golf to be a fascinating game.

Okay. I admit it is rather silly, the amount of money and time I spend all in the effort to guide a small, white, dimpled ball into a 4.25" hole in the ground. But my fascination is engaged when no two games ever play the same, even when I play the same course. Each golf shot is different from the last, and I find myself one shot away from utter despair, and one shot away from absolute euphoria.

And so the journey goes.

It is also true the harder I try, the worse I do. And, as I confessed earlier, I work hard at doing something—anything. And golf is a something teasing me with a sense of progress as I do it.

This day I find myself on the third tee, looking at the flag marking the location of the cup 168 yards away. There is a tall Douglas Fir standing on the left side of the fairway that I must avoid. On the right there is a bank with tall grass where I've lost several of my small, white, dimpled balls.

"This time I will hit it straight and keep it off the bank," I tell myself in an effort to will the ball to my target.

I have come to the course to play by myself today. I am worn out, weary from all of the chaos in my life, and I am searching for a "quiet place" where I might find even for a few moments, some relief from it all. I feel crowded by the chaos. I feel it pressing on me from all sides. Nothing seems to be working out. Life seems to be running out of control, nothing I do is helping, and I don't know where to turn.

My job life is in disarray. The work routine I have come to depend on is changing, as people who have become good friends are retiring, and the management structure is once again re-organizing, moving toward more control, demanding more results, and providing less support.

My home life is full of confusion. My kids have become young adults, leaving home, returning, and leaving again. My daughters have both moved hours away, and my son is in a relationship I think is unhealthy. It seems all of my efforts to help have only served to push him away. And in the middle of it all, my wife and I are wondering what we are to do now. I told her we need to get some counseling.

And so it goes.

I feel like I am coming undone. My life is a mess.

And so I have come to this golf course to get away from it all, to play a game, hoping I might find a few brief moments of relief. A few hours where I can simply be concerned with hitting and finding a small white dimpled ball, and perhaps here, alone on the course I can find a few moments to escape from the chaos and confusion before it overwhelms me.

This brings me back to the tee box of this third hole looking to the flag positioned 168 yards away, and my attempt to convince myself that this time I will not slice my shot into the tall grass on the bank.

This time I will hit it onto the green.

I step up to the ball, position my feet, adjust my grip on the five iron. I fix my gaze on the dimple I want to hit and look one last time at the flag, then back to the ball to begin my swing. Attempting to keep all the elements of motion synchronized in a determined effort to hit the ball to the green where I want it to land, I make my golf swing.

As the ball leaves the tee it looks to be on target. Maybe this time I will hit the green. But no—once again the ball curves to the right, landing on the bank in the grass and beyond the white-out of bound stakes.

Disappointed, I tee up a second ball and make the shot I wanted to hit the first time; this time, for some unknown reason I easily hit the green.

Now, there are two bad things that just happened. I incurred a penalty for myself by missing the first shot. The second bad thing is I might have lost my ball.

I hate losing my ball.

Typically I play with used balls (ones I've found while looking for others I've lost) or recycled golf balls purchased at the pro shop. Out of character and in an effort to improve my game, I made a purchase of new balls, never before struck by a golf club.

Finding little comfort in the fact I made a good second shot, I began to trod down the cart path to see if I could retrieve my first shot and at least suffer only a penalty shot, rather than adding a lost ball to the disappointment.

As I walk I look up to see an old man looking to be in his seventies, dressed in overalls and a blue shirt heading down the path towards me. He seems to have "appeared" from the tee box on the next hole; he has no clubs with him, and is out of place with his hands in his pockets, shuffling down the path towards me.

I quicken my pace just a bit in a futile attempt to get to the grassy bank where my first ball landed before this old farmer. He may be slower, but he has the advantage coming from the opposite direction. As he approaches the bank where my ball landed he pauses, steps up into the grass, bends over and picks up my ball and resume his walk in my direction.

"Did that happen to be Top Flight number three you just picked up?"

He reached into his pocket and pulled out the ball. "Yup" he replied putting my ball back into his pocket.

"Well, that'd be my ball," I said, smiling a bit, hoping to the ease the growing tension. "I just hit it and was coming to get it."

"Nope. You're playing. You don't get to look for balls if you're playing."

What? I think to myself. I can't believe this is happening.

"I just hit it there. I was coming to get it!" I was arguing my case with the old farmer.

"You can't play and look for balls at the same time." He stated, and continued his shuffle down the path.

My disbelief began to give way to anger, as I realized this old man had no intention of giving me my newly purchased Top Flight number three. He had no reply and offered no excuse for his offense.

He was stealing my ball in open defiance of my ownership.

I am not a man given to anger. It is not that I don't get angry. I simply don't know what to do with it when I do get angry. It does not make sense to give way to rage and make a mess that only requires me to clean it up afterwards. Perhaps I have concluded it is simply easier to deal with life if I give no favor to anger.

In spite of my methods to manage my anger, I am now finding a growing agitation within me. Compounded by the frustration of my inability to manage my life and resolve the issues that are well beyond my control, now, on a course where the rules are meant to guide and protect me from this sort of violation, an old man appears out of nowhere and steals my brand new golf ball!

'I bet I can take this old man! I can wrestle the ball out of his pocket! Farmer's are typically pretty strong, but I bet I can take him!' The thoughts race through my head, urging and restraining me at the same time.

It's only a ball!

*That's not the point! It's my ball, not his! He has no right to take
my new ball that I paid for and rightfully is mine!*

*It cost you a buck twenty-five! You're going to fight an old man
for a ball that cost a buck twenty-five?*

Concluding it was simply not worth a fight, I simply could
not let him go that easily. Turning to him again, this time my
voice raised making no attempt to ease tension or hide my
agitation.

"You don't even let a guy get a chance to hunt for his ball!
What the heck are you out here for anyway? You have no
business on this course!"

Bewildered, amazed, and confused, I turned away to process
what was happening to me and walked to the green and the
putt that was waiting for me. Confused and still angry, it
took me four putts to complete hole that was meant to take
three strokes from the tee box. I turned my gaze once again
to the cart path where the old farmer was walking, and he
was no longer there.

Irritated.

Angry.

Frustrated.

I teed up a ball on the fourth tee and proceed to slice it well
out of play.

Oh *%^#! Slow down. Compose yourself. Take a deep breath.

I proceed to tee up a second ball. Pausing for a moment I take a deep breath, exhale, look at my target and hit a good drive well positioned in the fairway for the next shot.

What is this? An old man out of nowhere, walks down the cart path, picks up my ball, steals it in front of my face, and walks away, seeming to disappear into thin air.

Angels appear and disappear.

Was that an angel? Did you send an angel down here to steal my ball and harass me? Don't I have enough trouble to deal with, and now you've sent a degenerate angel dressed like an old man to harass me! This may not be a revelation to You, but I'm angry. Furthermore, I don't think you're doing such a good job at taking care of things here! What is this with my life? It's coming undone. Right in front of my face, my life is coming undone, and I'm not sure you even care! My problems may not seem all that big to you, and sure there are plenty of people with bigger problems than I have, but that's not the point! These are my problems. They are what I am dealing with. I have to face them, and things are simply not working out here! And you don't seem to be paying attention. They just don't seem to matter to you!

I continued to play the course, turning my rage in full force toward God and no longer an old man in overalls. The incident with the old man had pushed me beyond the fear and usual restraints that would never allow me to address God in such a fashion. But now, I simply pushed those aside and turned to face God with all of my rage.

Deep emotions are not always visible from the outside. Perhaps I simply don't know how to express them all that well, but no one could possibly see the turmoil boiling within me. I was full of emotion as raw as I'd ever known and I was venting my anger and frustration to God, holding little to nothing back.

Hole after hole I played, continuing my rant, expressing my displeasure over each and every unresolved issue I faced.

Arguing with God was unfamiliar to me, and it felt more than a little dangerous, but I had come to the end of myself. Venting my dissatisfaction with how He was handling my life between shots and gritting my teeth to kill my irritation by taking it out on the small, white, dimpled ball, I worked my way around the course.

I found little pleasure in the game, as I argued through the next seven holes. On the eleventh hole I sliced my ball into the right edge of the fairway only to watch it bounce once into the tall grass. I had been in that knee high grass before, and it "eats" golf balls. Adding to my frustration, I simply considered this one gone.

My ranting was interrupted by a voice in my head.

Why don't you ask me to help you find that ball?

You don't care about that ball! You don't care about the issues in my life that I have to deal with, and you don't care about me! Why would I ask you for help with a stupid ball?

Ask me to help you find it.

I don't think so.

I teed up another ball, making a second attempt to hit a playable lie, only to watch this ball bounce into the same tall grass a few yards from my first shot.

Tired and dejected, I give in to the tall grass and walked to where I last saw the two balls bounce. Arriving at my reference point on the grass edge, I peer into the knee deep grass and weeds against all hope to perhaps find and reclaim one of the lost balls.

There, in plain sight lay a golf ball. A few yards away was the second, both of them mine. Tall grass that has swallowed and claimed far more golf balls then it has given up had left these two out in the open.

I was humbled.

In the midst of my ranting, and undaunted by my defiance to simply ask Him to help, even when He prompted me, He chose to show up in a small act of compassion to give me both of these two white balls back. I turned and dropped one of the found balls nearby to continue my play.

The argument within me just a few moments ago was finished.

There was no more turmoil to fuel it.

No rebuttal was offered to my complaints.

The anger within me was simply gone.

It was over.

It may not make any sense to you as you read this account. A silly game, small, dimpled balls, and an old man on a golf course— but my life was wrapped up in this ridiculous unfolding of seemingly innocuous events. I didn't expect to be undone as I was. I didn't expect the flood of emotions and the subsequent exposure of the feelings I was trying so hard to tame. Nor did I fully understand the sudden change within me.

The only explanation I can offer for the calm that overtook me is my anger simply had no more fuel. For some reason beyond my understanding or comprehension, God showed up in my chaos. He didn't show up to solve my problems or take them away and make everything happy. The issues of my life no longer weighed on me as they did a few moments ago. They were not gone. I still faced each one of them. For some unexplainable reason, I simply knew I was being taken care of. Life would work out. Not because of my efforts, but simply because God showed up in the midst of my ranting.

I was also humbled because—

I didn't get struck with lighting.

There was no stern correction.

And I received no lecture on anger management.

What is that I hear? Is that faint sound in my soul the belly laugh of God?

It's all part of the story

We each have a story, the unfolding of all the events, the mishaps and celebrations, the people, the places, and the time in which all of us live. These are the forces that have formed our interests, influenced our thoughts, and the perspectives we hold to. All of it, even those things we have suffered—the sin we have committed and the sin that has been committed against us—all of it together is what makes up the story of our lives.

This is the story we tell and the song we sing to the world; the time, the place, and the people who are part of our journey.

This writing, this book is all about searching to find life. If I have any hope of finding the fulfillment I long for, I will only find it as I live my story. I must learn the words to my song and how to sing it in the midst of the chaos and confusion in this journey that is my life.

My confusion is born of how I can possibly find life in a journey filled with so many bad things, some more dreadful than others. How does life happen in the midst of or in the aftermath of tragedy?

The story of the Phoenix rising from the ashes is inspiring, but what am I to do with the pain of the fire and the death that precedes the resurrection?

What am I to do with the shame?

How do I pick up the pieces of life and continue with any story at all?

Much of my story is embarrassing to me. I simply don't want anyone to know it.

Yet, these are the events that have shaped me. They have left their marks, even scars that have twisted and bent me into who I am. They have influenced how I view my world and the person I have become.

Many of these events serve as the milestones in my journey, reminding me of where I've been and from where I've come. In shaping me and bending me, they have become my story.

Let me illustrate how these events bend and twist us with another story. Even events seemingly benign can leave lasting marks upon our soul.

This story takes place in fifth grade, over forty years ago now, yet I still recall many of the details as if it had happened last month. I believe it was a day in March, and I remember sitting in the third row from the front, in the middle right of the room. We had the metal tub desks with the Formica lid that opened for storage of our school supplies. The chairs were plastic, and you could only easily sit down and get up from the left side of the desk.

The front room wall was covered by two large chalk boards with the metal tray running along the bottom to hold the chalk and erasers. The teacher's desk was front left. I still remember his name and face very well.

On this particular day we had been given an assignment, to draw a straight line using our ruler on a sheet of paper. Opening the lids of our desks, each of us retrieved our ruler and a clean sheet of paper to complete the assignment.

I was intent on making my line straight. I firmly held my ruler, pressing my left hand thumb and forefinger on the straight edge and began to draw the line at my thumb. At eleven-years-old my stretch equaled about six or seven inches of my twelve-inch ruler.

I firmly pressed the pencil against the straight edge. My line was straight until the pencil passed my forefinger placed at about the six-inch mark. In my attempt to make my line perfect I was pressing the pencil too hard against the ruler. As the pencil passed my finger on the six inch mark and moved beyond the seven inch mark, the pressure against the ruler became too great for my finger to hold it. The pressure I was putting on the ruler pushed it away and I was left with a seven inch straight line followed by a curved swoosh that bent towards the top of the paper.

As I made my attempt to draw my line, the teacher passed by my desk and witnessed my foiled attempt at a straight line.

What happened next is what etched this memory into my soul and helped shape who I am today. After witnessing my vain attempt to draw a simple straight line, the teacher had gone to the blackboard taking the yard stick from the chalk tray and holding it against the chalk board, turned to the class and said. "This is how McCoy draws a straight line." and exaggerated my failed attempt for all to see.

Time slowed to a halt for me as I sat in my desk. I don't remember anyone in the class laughing. I don't remember what happened next. I don't remember much of anything at that point.

I simply hung my head in humiliation and shame, feeling stupid and incompetent.

Now, in no way am I trying to equate this experience with some of the evil that has been committed on and to others. There simply is no comparison. I suffered no loss of life and the violation of my person may have been degrading, but I suffered no physical violence. There are daily reports and many that go unreported of events bearing a much greater brunt force in degrading a person than my experience in fifth grade.

What I am trying to say is that this event influenced the direction of my life, my story. It had a significant impact on how I manage the chaos of life. There was little rational thought behind my conclusion. It was far more a defensive decision, one in which I decided that from that time forward, to the best of my effort, I would do what I could to avoid looking stupid and feeling the humiliation of my stupidity ever again.

Over the years, I have developed many techniques that I still use in my effort to avoid looking stupid. Sometimes they have helped, and other times they have not. In my soul, I still harbor a fear of looking stupid.

As a result, I have spent a good deal of time trying to understand things.

I try to understand technology.

I try to understand people.

I read.

I think about things.

I listen and I observe.

In my effort to avoid looking stupid I have learned a great deal. I have become who I am and developed skills I would not have without the effort. The point is that events, some far more painful and deadly than my attempt at drawing a straight line, and some far less threatening, but none-the-less important to us, are the influences that serve to shape our lives and make us who we are.

They mark us. They pierce our hearts with deadly aim.

It feels like death.

And the response most often is, whatever the cost, we must protect ourselves, lest we die. The events are different for each of us but the results are much the same even though we choose different methods of protection.

We are determined to protect ourselves.

This evil we suffer, especially that which is intentional, is often committed by someone we know and trust, is beyond understanding. It is evil, and, whether intentional or unintentional it is still evil.

There is a God in Heaven, and He is in charge. I am not God, and I am not in charge. And the events that attempt to destroy me do fall under the control of a God who is in charge. I may be confused about the why, but He promised that these events that attempt to destroy me will be used as part of the story He is writing in my life and His purposes for me. If I really believe that, if that is all true, then I must wrestle life from the confusion and chaos and find the courage to face these "events" and understand at least a little of how they changed my course, and how they have influenced my story.

I want my life to be a song of celebration, not a funeral dirge. I don't want to trudge through life crippled by the damage I have endured, inflicted by others or myself. I want to learn to celebrate my story. It is easy for me to hear the pain of your story and celebrate your courage and success in living it. It is another account altogether when I must face my own pain and work through my chaos. I would rather leave old pain and suffering asleep where they lay, rather than face them to remember the hurt in order to make peace with them. I really don't want to relive them. And my feeble courage is easily overcome by the fear of additional sorrow. It is far too difficult to integrate the painful events of life into my story.

Yet I must face them if I am to claim my life for celebration and not allow life to be lived as if it were a funeral progression. Maybe this is what Jesus is talking about when He says we are to die to ourselves.[8] Maybe He is asking us to die to the efforts of trying to protect ourselves, thinking life is found in defending ourselves rather than in celebrating in the tapestry of events that work together to create in us glory, splendor, beauty and wonder.

Your events are not mine, and my events are not yours; your methods of protection are likely to be different than mine. Like it or not, each of us own our events and our methods. Both have served to influence the course of our lives, the decisions we make and the directions we take. Our events have shaped our story. They have become the melody of the song we sing, a dirge or an anthem.

Paul's words now mean so much more to me when he says that "All things work together for good to those who love God." [9]

Ten

Change Management

"There is but one good; that is God. Everything else is good when it looks to Him and bad when it turns from Him."—C.S. Lewis

Confession—the prerequisite to change

I have wondered many times what it might have been like to have been in the Garden with Adam and Eve. In my imagination, I picture it as a warm and friendly place with tropical plants and lush grass, complimented by a warm sweet fragrance in the air. I imagine plenty to eat with little effort, no traffic, no taxes, no meetings, no cell phones, and no fear.

Then I wonder why Adam and Eve chose to eat the fruit of the forbidden tree instead of eating the fruit from the tree of Life.

They had it. Right there in front of them. Life; hanging from the tree, ready to be eaten, right there for them.

There were no prohibitions to partaking of life; the only prevention was the muscle effort required to reach up and take it. But they chose knowledge instead of life. It was their only restriction, the only limit requested of them, and they chose to ignore the warnings, only to discover shame and guilt as they ingested the forbidden fruit of knowledge.

And then they hid.

And that is exactly what all of us have been doing ever since. We hide.

We don't hide in the bushes. We've learned that God does not have any trouble finding us in the bushes. So we hide in other places.

I read Einstein once remarked it is impossible to solve a problem by using the same type of thinking that created the problem in the first place. But that is exactly what I do, I continue to try and solve my problems using the same thinking that got me into them in the first place.

I hate the fact I can't get it right. I hate my failures. I hate my sin and what it leaves me with.

I'd like to change, but I don't know how to do it any differently. When I try and get myself out of it, I use the same thinking that got me into the problem in the first place. It simply doesn't work. What is there left to do?

And so I hide.

In the same fashion as Adam and Eve, I look desperately for someplace where I am not exposed. A place where I am covered and do not have to face the shame of my failure. I hide by letting others take responsibility so I do not have to. I hide by avoiding situations that will expose me, where others might see me for who I really am. I hide by blaming others and pointing out their failures so that perhaps mine will go unnoticed.

When finally there is no place for me to hide from others, I hide from myself by doing something, anything just so I can be distracted by the activity—whatever it takes to keep the focus somewhere else—anywhere but on me.

And God asks me to believe.

He invites me to come to Him, trusting that He is true, right, fair, and honest. And that He loves me more than I can comprehend. He only asks for one thing in return:

He wants me to quit hiding.

He calls it confession.

He asks me to come out of hiding and admit to the things I have done that have hurt me and alienated Him. He wants me to admit I have let him down, to admit to the clever schemes I have used as a substitute to satisfy my thirst. My thirst which is really for Him.

Go and sin no more
Let me tell you what I know about horses.

My wife grew up with horses. She didn't have a farm where she could keep and care for a horse, but somehow she was able to buy a horse and keep it in a pasture a few minutes away from her house. Her affection for horses began well before she owned one as she spent hours as a child watching the neighbor girl ride and groom her horse.

I had never thought much, one way or the other, of horses. I rode motorcycles as a boy.

As our children grew up, we had neither motorcycles nor horses. A few years after my daughter got her first horse, my wife purchased a horse for herself and began to learn much more about training and teaching a horse. We attended a local horse expo where we met John Lyons, who is a world renowned horse trainer. He is such a great teacher even I learned some things about horses.

John taught me about round pens. The interesting thing about a round pen is there is no corner for the horse to run to and hide. He also taught me that horses get very nervous if you simply look at their hind quarters. It makes them feel threatened.

Horses don't have sharp claws and big teeth. Somehow they don't know that steel shoes have been nailed to the bottom of their feet and they weigh about ten times what I weigh. And so what they do when they feel threatened is run.

If they are in a round pen, they run in circles.

This makes it very convenient for the trainer who can now stand in the middle of the round pen and watch the horse run in circles. A horse's natural response to fear is to get away from what frightens them.

So they run.

Watching John Lyons working with a horse that had never been ridden or saddled was fascinating for me. Here was a good ol' bow-legged cowboy with his hand in his pocket in a round pen with a horse so neurotic it would jump and run from the reaction of the audience. I found myself thinking that his goal of riding the horse in two hours might be more than a little optimistic, especially because the horse was not in the least interested in getting near John.

Intrigued, I watched as John would look at the hindquarters and wave a rope to direct the horse's fear. It was no problem to get the horse to run and John was doing more than he could explain to us as he watched, directed, and ran the untrained animal in circles.

Every few minutes, John would turn his attention from the horse to the audience and the horse would pause for a moment to turn and look at John.

This was a round pen. There were no corners for the horse to hide in, and there was no escape from the pen. The horse had no way to get away from John.

My wife has since taught me that while John was talking, he was working to get the horses attention. He does this by watching the horses head. When John works with a horse in the round pen, he pressures the horse by looking at the hind quarters and watches the head, waiting for the horse to turn its head toward its fear. When the horse moves so much as an ear in John's direction, John will release the pressure by turning his gaze away from the horse's hind quarters and the horse will stop running. Over time this builds the horses trust in John.

That is an illustration of what God is like.

When I read the Bible and the things Jesus says to people, I am often left confused.

Many times what Jesus says simply doesn't make sense to me.

A good example is the scene in the street where the religious men dragged a sexually promiscuous woman to Jesus. I like how Jesus handled the men who had gathered stones, ready to kill the woman for her sin, putting Jesus to a test, thinking they were forcing Him to lead them in her execution per the Law of Moses. He seems to easily diffuse the situation by simply offering the first blow to the man who could say he was without sin.

After they all leave, He has a short conversation with the woman, His final words to her are, "Go and sin no more." [10]

What does that mean?

What was Jesus telling this woman?

What did He mean when He told her to "sin no more"?

Certainly He meant for her to quit her futile attempt to find love and life through her promiscuous methods.

Was that all He meant? Doesn't it mean exactly what it says?

Doesn't it also mean that Jesus wants her to, in every aspect of her life to stop her rebellion toward God and stop sinning?

No sin.

No more.

Ever.

After years of attempting to "sin no more," I find His first request, to stop her adulterous ways possibly achievable. She might be able to change her behavior.

I find the second meaning, to stop all sin right now, to be an impossible request.

One conclusion is evident to me as I read about Jesus and how he responds to people; He understands us. He has a supernatural ability to see into our hearts and understand our fear and the hunger and thirst behind our actions. Jesus understood this woman, even if I don't understand His words to her.

I make no claims to understand people as well as Jesus, but I do know that this woman who was dragged from bed, with only her shame to cover her was not prepared to be in a public place. She was accused by angry religious people (and I expect a few of the properly dressed dignified men knew where she could be found, possibly having visited her bedroom themselves). Only now they used her for their religious pleasure instead of their personal pleasure.

I do not expect she lifted her eyes to face them, now her accusers, these angry religious leaders and Jesus. I picture a circle of properly dressed men, rocks in their hands looking at Jesus as she sat in the dirt, clutching to what she was able to grasp as she was snatched from a bedroom, using it as her only covering, attempting to hide behind her hands and perhaps a small cloth.

She was in a round pen with nowhere to hide. Jesus, in His ability to know her and see her heart, was watching her run and waiting for her to turn even an ear toward Him, waiting for her to give in to Him.

That is what Jesus does. He gets us in a round pen and lets us run until we are willing to turn to look at him.

I run to find what I think will make me happy, what I think will help me find life. I run because I am afraid, and so I run and run and run.

All the while Jesus is watching, waiting until I am willing to give Him an ear, to ever so slightly turn my head in His direction. Then, in his delight, He turns and lets me rest, satisfied I am beginning to look toward Him for life and venturing out of my hiding places.

I am so tired of running in circles.

Repentance: the first of the three R's

It was a Sunday morning, and I found a bee's nest in the birdhouse on the barn. Most of the nests I find are yellow jackets, more accurately called wasps than bees. I have no fondness for yellow jackets. I have been stung many times by them, and truth be told, I rather enjoy killing them. I think I'm rather good at it, and have developed several methods over the years to eliminate the troublesome pests.

This nest presented a problem because it was inside the birdhouse. I had attached the birdhouse to the barn using wooden screws, so in order to eliminate these wasps, I needed to get on the ladder and unscrew the birdhouse. So I put on my heavy overalls and a pair of heavy leather gloves. I taped the gloves to the sleeves and the pant legs to the top of my boots. I put a wide brim cowboy hat on and draped a loose knit sweater over my head so I could see through the knits.

I took my ladder and drill motor and climbed up to where I could reach the birdhouse. Insulted by my intrusion they began to buzz my head attempting to sting the sweater as I unscrewed the birdhouse. (You might be wondering why I didn't just buy a can of spray and kill them. Well, that required a trip to the store and six bucks. As I said earlier, I have developed many techniques to exterminate yellow jackets.) I knocked the birdhouse to the ground, climbed down the ladder and then uncovered my head.

Next I took a jar of gas and poured it into the opening that contained the nest. I have developed a method of throwing a lit match by using my thumb to strike the match and throw it in one smooth motion. I may have learned it after burning off my eyebrows in a similar experiment years earlier, and I used it again to keep both the burst of flames and the wasps away from me. Just as I let the lit match fly towards the nest, I noticed I had inadvertently thrown the nest into a pile of dry wood shavings my wife uses for bedding in the horse stall.

Usually this would not be a concern, as the water hose was just around the corner, but that morning, for some reason kept only to themselves, the city had turned the water supply all but off. This meant I would have a fire on my hands in a matter of minutes, and the water hose was currently of no use to me.

As the match performed its mission and the nest burst into flames, I ran to get a shovel and to see if I could coax some small amount of water out of the facet into a bucket. The facet apparently appreciating my predicament trickled a small amount of water into my bucket. Armed with what looked to be a quart of water and a shovel to smother it with dirt I ran back to the fire, which by now was fully consuming the nest and beginning to burn the wood shavings. The water dampened the material that did not have gas, and in a few moments I was able to smother the flames with the dirt.

It was then I noticed the "bees" were not the yellow jackets that I despise, but a type of Bumble Bee with an orange back.

These were useful pollinators to my raspberries and fruit trees. And I was immediately sorry for their destruction and wished I hadn't destroyed their nest. I took the charred nest, wet and dirty, and put it back into the birdhouse. Then moved the birdhouse to a place where the nest could be rebuilt if the remaining bees still flying around the remains took an interest and were able to salvage anything that was left.

I was sorry I killed the bees, but at this point there was nothing I could change to make a difference.

I had changed my mind but there was nothing more I could do.

All I could change was my mind.

I couldn't bring any of the bees back to life.

I couldn't rebuild their nest.

I looked at a few remaining bees flying around the empty space on the barn where the birdhouse was a few minutes ago. I couldn't tell them where I had moved the nest. (I still didn't want them on the barn!)

This is what John the Baptist was sent to tell the people in preparation for the coming Messiah. It was what Jesus told them when He began to preach to them. John and Jesus were telling them to change their mind.

Jesus and John were telling them their thinking had gotten them where they were, and they needed to change the way they were thinking if they were to make any progress toward life and happiness.

The word that John and Jesus used was *repent*.

They said, *repent*, which meant *change your mind, for the kingdom of God is at hand.*

Repentance is nothing more or less than changing your mind.

When you stop to think about it, there is nothing else you can really change.

If I want to change my eating habits, to eat better to enjoy better health, to lose weight or fight heart disease or digestive problems, I first have to change my mind. If I want to change the shape I'm in and start an exercise program, I must first change my mind.

If I want to change my work, my golf game, my marriage, my kids, or the car I own, the first thing I must do is to change my mind.

I'm not saying there is nothing any of us can do, or that all effort is fruitless. I am saying that anything we do and anything we wish to change begins with what we think. I am also saying there are some very important things about my life I would really like to change. These are things I don't like, things I wish I could do better, things I wish I didn't do at all, and I have no ability or power to change them or to fix them.

For those things I have done wrong, there are no "do-overs," as much as I wish there were. I am left with what I've done, with who I am, and knowing I would like to be different. I am left with the responsibility for my actions and the penalties involved. If the bees were insured and had a lawyer to represent them, I would have had to pay damages and legal fees for my actions.

It would be appropriate.

Very likely, I would have been requested to rebuild their house and relocate it on the side of the barn. However, all of my actions to help them recover would not have changed what happened, and the effort to restore the damage would be just that, an effort that could never replace or restore what I did.

My good intentions are not enough, and it would not be repentance. My efforts to repay them would be just and right. However appropriate my actions would be to help them recover, those actions do not necessarily represent a changed mind, a difference in my thinking.

When John the Baptist said "repent" he was telling the people they needed to change their minds.

Relinquishment: out of control
There is a God, and I am not Him.

That is what I have told many people. It is not original. I got it from a friend, but I like it, and so I use it as a simple explanation and reminder that I am not in control.

It is easy to say and very difficult for me to practice. Several years ago I had an occasion to do more than practice it. I had an opportunity to put it to work.

While traveling to Montana for a week of fishing and camping with my family and my brother's family, I realized I had lost my wallet on the on ramp to the freeway. The on ramp was some sixty minutes back down the road where we had just come from. In spite of the slim odds I would find it where I knew it had dropped, I had to return to the spot to see for myself, and know that my wallet was gone.

It just so happened during that specific time in my life, I had begun to wrestle with God's control over life in contrast to my responsibility to manage my life. I had read that if God is really in charge then He is in charge of everything. I read that if God was in charge, then there cannot be one renegade molecule in the universe, or God is not really in charge.

I remember the day I had begun to realize the implications of this, and I had laid awake in bed well into the morning hours, considering what it meant to me and life. I don't mean to make that a big deal. There have been many people much smarter than me, who have spent lifetimes wrestling with the implications of God's control in life. For me, I simply couldn't sleep for five or six hours as the truth of God's control began to invade my limited understanding of life and change the way I would be living it.

I unhitched the truck from the camp trailer leaving it and the kids with my brother and his family and my wife and I drove back to the on ramp where I had lost my wallet, echoing in my head were the words that *God is in complete control of all things in my life.* I was considering the fact that *nothing happens that He does not intend to happen or allow to happen.*

That is what it means to me that God is in charge.

As I approached the on-ramp where I hoped against the odds to find my wallet and recover my cash and credit cards, I was considering what it means to live a life in which I am not in control. Who *is* in control is someone who cares deeply for me, who can arrange every detail of my life to work *all things* out for my ultimate good; He is in control.

Then I stopped to look for my wallet, and it was nowhere to be found.

My wife and I retraced our path back to the family and the camp trailer we'd left behind to make the trip faster. The first indication I had of the personal significance of God being in charge was when my brother looked at me to assess my reaction to the situation. He was looking for a sign of how I would act out my frustration or anger at my loss, and after some interaction and evaluation, he said he thought I would have taken it harder.

Don't misunderstand. It was not a pleasant experience for me. I did not look forward to the hassle of stopping my credit cards, getting them replaced, replacing my driver's license, and I hated losing the cash I had planned to use on our family vacation. It was all a pain—part of my personal chaos.

I am not saying I had no responsibility in losing my wallet. It was my fault. I should have been more careful. I am saying the way I previously thought about life had begun to change, and I was beginning to think that God is in control of even these little things, and that He could have prevented it or allowed it.

In other words, I was changing my mind and learning to trust Him.

I no longer was required to punish myself for my ineptitude, my inability to manage life the way I thought it should be. God was in control, and I could trust Him with the future and perhaps learn to do better at taking care of my wallet.

I admit that letting go of this personal responsibility to punish myself was not easy to do. I had to fight the familiar feeling that I should be miserable for at least a few days. It seemed wrong to allow myself to enjoy the vacation when I had been so irresponsible in losing the money we had saved for this getaway.

Could I accept this as part of His plan for me?

This day? These failures? This chaos?

If He is really in control, then losing my wallet is no surprise to Him, and He said that He would work things out for me. Whether it was planned or permitted doesn't really matter.

What matters is whether I trust Him. Do I trust that He is in control, and that I no longer have to be?

I was changing my mind about how I live.

I was also learning a new word; relinquishment. As I changed my mind I was learning I could also give up control, or at least the pretense that I was in control. A few years later, I had another event that reinforced this new thinking, this changing of my mind, and the new concept of trusting that God is in charge of my life. I mentioned earlier I applied myself with a great amount of energy to getting life right. What I achieved was frustration and a low grade, underlying anger as a companion.

My job required me to set appointments, keep an extensive list of contacts, and track the activities pertaining to each contact. This was before laptop computers, and all of our calendars and schedules were all kept on paper—mine in a three ring binder. This binder contained my professional life. I referred to it as my brains because of the amount of information it held for me.

After one of my customer visits I was loading some equipment into the back of my station wagon. I didn't have the hands to manage everything, so I put my binder on top of the car. (You can see what's coming here can't you?)

I drove off without remembering my binder.

I was twenty minutes and ten miles away when I remembered. I spent the afternoon looking for any sign of my book. It was nowhere to be found.

I was devastated.

I felt it would have been easier for me to lose my job than to lose my binder with all of the information I used to help me determine where I needed to go next, who to contact, addresses, phone numbers and what I needed to talk to them about. I didn't know what I was supposed to do the next day. My book was most likely scattered in the ditch somewhere or in the hands of someone who should not have my personal information.

Once again I was faced with the futility of trying to manage and organize my life in light of my own ineptitude and inherent imperfection.

After hours of searching in vain, despair was the feeling I remember most as I drove home to face my family. It was clearly written on my face as I walked in the door to greet my young children and wife. After explaining my day and the story of losing and then frantically searching for my binder, they understood the look of despondency on my face. I began to drag myself up the stairs to my room to change out of my work clothes and into something more comfortable; it is my after-work ritual.

I had only taken a few steps up the stairs when my twelve year old son stopped me.

"Dad, you usually get pretty angry when these types of things happen. This time you didn't. That's pretty cool."

He had stopped me to talk, and now I stood stunned from his comments. I had no idea he could see into me with that much clarity. I was ashamed of the anger that I previously had been unable to control and wondered how much he and the rest of my family had had to endure, when I had thought my reactions had been subdued and managed.

But on this day, somehow in the process of simply changing my mind about who had real control in my life, somehow in the feeble efforts to relinquish my out-of -control life to One who is in control, somehow I was learning to trust.

And I was changing.

In front of the eyes of a child I had changed from an emotionally angry man to one my twelve-year-old son could find the courage to approach amidst a disaster, and speak to without fear.

Pretty cool, huh?

No. Not simply pretty cool.

Way cool.

Redemption: the power of honesty

I enjoy baseball. I started playing when I was eight years old. I continued playing into my forties. Since grade school, I try to watch the playoffs each fall.

As I watched the final game of the 2006 World Series in the midst of the Cardinal's celebration, they switched the camera to the obligatory interview with the coach of the losing team. The Tigers had lost in five games. They had fallen apart and their hopes and dreams of the World Series Championship title were now replaced by the disappointment of the loss. "We just didn't play well enough to win a World Series."

Coach Leyland's response had captured my attention. He is known as a straight shooter coach, and I was interested to see what more he might say. Most comments from the losing coach are predictable. You can expect them to congratulate the winning team, avoiding any talk of what they or their team might have done differently to have changed the outcome.

There had been eight unearned runs scored during the five games. They had been scored on errors that each pitcher committed in each game; eight runs that could have been the difference in one or more of the games that had handed the Tigers their defeat. Coach Leland was asked about the errors committed by the pitching staff. I was expecting to hear something about how they might work with the young pitchers, or in some oblique way, an acknowledgement of how the consecutive throwing errors cost them. But that is not what Leland did.

In fact, I was completely caught off guard by his comments. The honesty of what he said stunned me.

"I didn't get my team ready to play like I should have."

He didn't blame his players, but instead took responsibility for the loss. I've never heard an interview like this one. The interview was over as quickly as it had begun, so they could get back to the celebration of the Cardinals. Leland's words echoed in my ears for moments as I watched the corks fly and the bottles of Champaign poured and sprayed in celebration.

Coach Leyland's honesty had much more power than anything he could have offered to excuse or dismiss their failure.

Honesty is a power that can change the world. It has changed me when I was powerless and incapable of being any different.

I have spent many years trying to change, and I have come to understand through a nest of bees and a lost notebook that I am powerless to change much about who I am. It seems my power is mostly limited to the ability to change my mind; repentance and who I trust; relinquishment.

I am so tired of running in circles.

I've found the way out of the round pen is honesty. Honest about the places I have chosen to hide. Honesty about when I am hiding, and then being willing to turn, look to Him, and stop running —trusting that He is always good. Always.

I am no longer the angry man my son knew as a young boy. I am free from a good deal of the low grade anger that accompanied me throughout much of my life. Through the honesty and changing of my mind, I am returning to the spirit I remember as a young boy. I am coming closer to the man I believe I was created to be.

It is the final R—redemption.

In my honesty, I've had to admit I don't even posses the ability to keep track of my wallet. I am in need of someone much more capable than myself if I am to navigate this life of chaos and confusion, someone much bigger and more capable than you or me.

I have found that my failure, even my intentional rebellion, when faced with the honesty of admission, moves me toward the changes that I welcome.

Honesty is releasing me from having to pretend I'm tough, strong, capable, or competent—when I'm *not*. Honesty is enabling me to be strong, capable, and competent—when I *am*—and not have to hide in either situation. Honesty is restoring within me strength in place of the resentment and weakness bred by denial and blame.

Honesty has given me the courage to look to the center of the round pen, the courage to look the trainer in the eyes. It is in His eyes that I have discovered the acceptance I've always wanted.

And He's not mad at me for running in circles.

Eleven

What's Love Got To Do With It?

"Any time that is not spent on love is wasted."—Torquato
Tasso

What do you mean?
I've been married for over half of my life.

I've told you about being a teenager and my desire to find a
young woman with whom I could share my life, someone
who would be interested in discovering life together. I have
distinct memories of that time and the effort it took to hold
onto a hope of finding such a partner. More often than not
the hope of finding someone seemed to be a far-away,
unreachable hope, filled with more fantasy than reality. As
always, the future offered nothing certain with the exception
of having to face it, and there was little to relieve my fear of
having to face it on my own—alone.

My thoughts at that time went something like this:

*Is that what life holds for me? Is that what I have to look forward
to, alone? How do I know if there is someone for me? Could there
possibly be an attractive young girl that would enjoy my*

company, and I could enjoy hers—someone who would want to be my soul mate, my partner, and companion in this journey of life?

Does she even exist?

These were the nature of my questions and the fuel for much of my apprehension about the future. It was in the ninth grade, my last year of junior high, one of my English teachers took our class to see the newly released movie, *Romeo and Juliet*. What a great way to get out of class! It didn't matter what the movie was, but then I found myself awe-struck with Juliet. Her beauty captivated me. Most certainly it was how she looked, but more than her eyes, more than her long flowing hair, her strong cheek bones and her cleavage, I think I was captivated by the love she had for Romeo, and the love he had for her.

A story set in a different time with different values and customs. A story of conflict, anger, and hatred between two families, and a story of a great passion and love between two naive young people that transcended the time, the customs, and all of the condescension and hate.

That was what I was looking for. I wanted that kind of passion. I longed for that kind of love—a love that could transcend all of the chaos in my life. A love that so deeply infected me it would fuel my passion for living, my incentive to build and provide, and would merit giving my life for.

A love that more than promises life. I was searching for a love that births life by its very existence.

This was a movie, actors speaking their parts on queue and acting out the scenes as written. Is that kind of love even possible? I didn't know, but wanted to find out if it might be possible for me. Leaving the theater, I was left with little more than a renewed ache in my stomach that only reminded me of the thirst in my soul. My experience may well have been typical of a ninth grader—thirsty yet not quite knowing how to quench the thirst. Then again it may not be typical, as the insecurities of ninth graders were never spoken or said aloud. My questions and confusion may have been common for the others or they may have belonged to me alone.

Whatever the case, I would not have been able to put words to my feelings at the time. I may have been able to put words to them if the words were given to me, but I am very confident the words would never have been spoken by me. What I did know at that time is that this story of two young lovers, very near my age, this story written some four hundred years ago, in a time and place I will never fully understand, had captured my emotions and deeply moved me.

I wandered my way through the rest of ninth grade and on into high school, finally reaching the glory of graduation, thirteen years after leaving behind the thrill of kindergarten. I suppose you could say I was fully engaged in shopping for my Juliet at this point of my life. As I would meet young women of my age, I would ponder the possibilities as to whether this might turn into the one relationship in which the both of us could find this passion and devotion that Romeo and Juliet demonstrated. Could this be one with whom we could both grow together, pursuing dreams, and living a life that would be full, rich, and alive?

I remember dating my future bride and asking myself the questions as we enjoyed simply being together. We talked for hours, the conversation flowing with little effort. We could sit and listen to music or just be together. And we enjoyed it all, because we were together.

I remember.

I also remember the early years of our marriage. They say that men lose their mind after the wedding. Perhaps that is exactly what happened. The effortless conversation that flowed so easily turned into so much work we would give up on it altogether at times. A constant agitation and discontent seemed to be the norm for our relationship.

I discovered new hiding places to escape the chaos. This was not the relationship that I thought it would be. This was not what I had dreamed about while watching Romeo and Juliet in ninth grade.

My young wife and I began to form new patterns where we would ebb and flow toward and away from each other. There were times when we would force the dialogue, wondering sometimes aloud at what happened to the two people we knew before our wedding. I remember talking to God about the relationship, convinced He had made a mistake; certainly the confusion of this relationship was not what He had in mind when He said that two would become one.

How is it two people can so totally understand each other before they are married, and have so much misunderstanding once the wedding vows have been exchanged? Sometimes when things were difficult, when the frustration seemed overwhelming, one of us would turn to the other and say, "I love you." Often it was a courageous and brave statement, given the chaos and distance in the relationship. And it was heartfelt.

I found times when those three little words, "I love you" were terribly difficult to speak, not because they weren't true. I just wasn't sure what the words meant anymore.

What does "I love you" really mean?

What am I trying to tell her when I say to her that I love her? And what does it mean when she says she loves me? Am I telling her that I need her? Am I telling her that she looks attractive to me, and I want her to be the fulfillment of my dreams? Does it mean I want something more from her? Am I telling her that I still want her for my wife, and I haven't given up yet? Am I simply telling her I want to jump in bed with her?

What does it mean?

I expect more words have been written about love than any other subject or theme on earth. There are more songs, more movies, and more poems about love than I can count. There are songs that proclaim undying love. A love that will swim the oceans or climb the mountains

What does climbing a mountain or swimming an ocean prove?

I've heard songs boasting that "you were made for me."

And I wonder, what if she didn't think I was made for her?

There are songs that proclaim "your love is my salvation."

Am I her salvation? And what happens if she takes her love away?

Am I lost?

Some songs simply say I want to have sex with you have confused love with simple lust, degrading the partner into an object. It seems to me the songs I hear are focused mostly about me and what I get from the deal, and very little consideration is given about her needs or what she gets from the relationship. How does that work? How can she and I get together, hoping to meld our hopes and dreams together and reach for those dreams, if we are not considering each other, but are only pursuing our own needs?

How does love work?

Do I expect her to share my dreams and give up hers? Does she expect me to fill her dreams and lose my own?

After listening to so many songs on love I now know I can make my needs, demands, and even my lust sound very attractive and smart when I put them to a catchy beat with a moving melody and croon them as love. So what does love look like? Does it really look like Romeo and Juliet? After all, they didn't have to live together. In their story, they had the easy part, enjoying all of the infatuation and passion before the wedding. Then before they ever had to deal with which way to squeeze the toothpaste, or who would take out the garbage, pay the bills, earn a living, or whose family they would visit this Christmas, they ended their lives.

Frankly they are a bad example for me to follow.

Yet in the face of the reality and all of the disappointment in love, there is an irrepressible hope within me that I might do much more than find love. I want to live in it, to discover its passion and be changed for the better from the experience. It may not be the reality I know, but it is the love I want to know and the life I long for.

Of course life and living is all about relationships and love depends on relationship, a deep connection to another person. Because relationship is the cornerstone of love, I must learn about relationship. I must learn about relating to other people to better learn about finding life.

Relationships: the birth of life

My father-in-law, Ron Ingram, was a retired navy Lieutenant, a Viet Nam veteran, and a Merchant Marine. He spent months at sea. He was a tough sailor; hard, stubborn, and guided by an unbreakable code of honor. The first time I met him was in my driveway on a Sunday afternoon. He and my mother-in-law had just arrived from the Philippines. We knew they were coming, but didn't know when, and we didn't know they planned on staying with us.

A few years later this retired military officer told me he thought I was a hippy when we first met. It may have been my long hair and my bell bottom jeans, or it may have been simply who I was. Whatever the differences behind our lack of relationship, it took several years for us to learn about each other and build a relationship of mutual respect. Time, experience with each other, and grandkids helped us both. Relationships were not all that easy for him, and to this day they are still a mystery to me.

After he retired from the Merchant Marines, he purchased a local tavern. It was his dream. I suppose it was his dream because it provided him a place to drink and work and he enjoyed doing both. It may have simply been a comfortable place for him to hide from the confusion in his own broken life.

Whatever the motivation, it was a lifestyle choice that would prove to be his undoing. I am sure his choice was made in part because he was most comfortable in that kind of environment, and he could dictate the tone of the relationships in a tavern that he owned. To say he handled the patrons on his terms would be a bit of an understatement. Those that offered him no trouble he would leave them to enjoy their drink at their table. The ones he didn't think much of or who caused him any trouble, he would simply run them off. He was known to do so on a number of occasions.

One old-timer, surprised by how much kinder he was treated when he was alone in the bar asked him why he was so rude to him when other people were around. Ron answered by simply shrugging his shoulders and saying, "Just cause." The old-timer said he didn't think Ron liked him until the others left.

I felt much the same as the old-timer.

It took a little over a decade before the choices extracted their toll on Ron. He had been hospitalized twice for major surgery, and was recovering from the second surgery in a cabin on a river in the mountains when he told my wife he wanted me to come up and see his place. His request puzzled me. I was unsure of why he might want me to visit, but was happy to take the time to make the trip to his cabin. When we arrived I could see in his face and his actions the great delight he had in showing me the old house and his view of the river.

It was that day I realized Ron liked me. I had thought he simply tolerated me before, but after that visit I knew he really liked me.

A few weeks later, he returned to the hospital. It had become an all too familiar routine to us, but not a routine that would continue for much longer. My wife and I called our kids to make what we expected would be their last visit to Grandpa. He wasn't able to speak much, so we each took a turn to tell him about our recent events and accomplishments, including our feeble attempts to comfort him and let him know we loved him.

My turn came last. I don't remember anything of what I told him. What I do remember is telling him I'd like to pray for him. It wasn't the first time I had prayed for him in a hospital bed, so I braced myself a bit as I made my request.

Praying wasn't something the old sailor liked very much. The slight grimace and the blank stare on his face as if he were in some grave pain were what gave him away. It was as if he was hardening himself against my prayer with tolerant disdain. Yes, disdain is a good word to describe the expression I was met with. I had only prayed with him during his hospital stays, and disdain was how he had endured the gesture during previous visits, all the while keeping his eyes open and holding that blank stare, as he was looking off into the distance at nothing in particular, while he waited for it to be over.

As I anticipated his response to my intention to pray for him I was uncertain as to whether it would increase his discomfort or add to the emotional agony he was suffering as he laid there, his body slowly deteriorating. I certainly did not wish to add to his unpleasant situation, but sometimes I know I am supposed to do something, and this was one of those times. All I wanted was to help him somehow, to maybe ease some of his pain. Since I had no ability to make a difference in his health and no ability to defer his pain, the only resource left to me was to make a personal request to God on his behalf.

As I began my prayer, waiting for the same reaction I had received as before, I left my eyes open and continued to look

Ron in the eye as I began a conversation with God. I put my hand on his shoulder and began.

"God, here we are, and Ron is not well. I would like you to help him. You can touch him and make him well again, but you don't often do that sort of thing. I would like him to know, in all of this, how much you love him and how much we love him, and that he might find some hope and life in you."

Looking at my father-in-law I was not met with the stiff expression I was expecting, the one he had given in the past. It wasn't there this time. The blank stare was replaced by an unfamiliar softness. He joined me this time. His eyes held mine, and they welcomed me. There was a look of gratitude in his face as I finished.

As I was saying my goodbye, I told him I'd see him again. What happened next was beyond unexpected to me.

This crusty old sailor took my hand and kissed it, agreeing he would see me again with a nod and a smile.

I had no words as he held my hand close to his face, not wanting to let it go. My eyes welled up as I held back tears. All I could do was stand there, feeling helpless and useless as I choked back my tears.

A few days later he returned to the house on the river where he passed shortly after. We held his memorial in the Tavern, where patrons remembered the stubborn man that served them, never really sure of his feelings toward them.

I wish I'd known him better.

I wish I'd spent more time with him.

I wish I'd had more courage to enter into his life and share mine with him.

The experience left me wanting to get to know other people better, before we get to the memorial part of their journey. To somehow discover the person underneath the surface, to discover the splendor beneath their facade before it's too late.

I've changed some. But frankly, I still haven't changed all that much.

Why are relationships so hard?

Why do we take so many of them for granted until they are gone?

Tattoos and brotherhood

I've heard a man might be able to find a handful of friends in a lifetime. I don't know if it applies to woman as well, but I think they were right.

I am a fortunate man in that I have had my handful. One of my friends, Rory, I met in high school, and we were reacquainted when we purchased Harley's in our late forties. We began to plan rides together, and I became friends with Glenn, Rory's long-time friend from grade school.

It is pretty common that patches and tattoos come with the Harley culture. Rory and Glenn decided to get a tattoo of a Chinese word meaning brotherhood. They wear it and share it with great pride. They are friends that have become brothers and have a heart and dedication to each other that is hard to find.

During one of our rides Glenn offered me an invitation that caused me to pause. He said, "Steve, Rory and I talked about it, and we'd be proud if you wanted to share this tattoo with us."

It was one of the most meaningful and generous invitations I had ever received. Due to an incident in third grade, I simply avoid needles. Frankly, I am afraid of them. Because needles are the method used for tattoos, it has not been a form of expression I have ever considered, that is until Glenn's invitation.

Rory mentioned to me during a conversation with Glenn, Glenn asked him if he thought I would ever get the tattoo. "No," he said. "It's tattooed on his heart."

I was grateful on two counts. Because I was afraid of needles, I was grateful I didn't have to get the tattoo, and I was grateful for my acceptance into their brotherhood. We had become close friends. They are two of a few men with whom I somehow have a connection of the heart. I guess you could say we have relationship.

It is not that we are the same or share the same ideas or lead similar lives. We don't. We are different in many ways. I think what we share is an acceptance of each other's differences and an appreciation of what each of us offers to the relationship. It is not simply tolerance, putting up with each other.

We enjoy each other's company. We are each grateful for the relationship.

I also have two brothers by birth as well. Somehow in the journey to adults we grew to enjoy each other, playing together and depending on each other. I'm not sure how it happened to us, it just did.

One dark Monday evening in late November, my youngest brother Kev called me. He simply said, "We have a problem." Now my first thought was what problem did he have that could be of such magnitude that it was mine as well. Then he said, "Tim went over the bank."

I immediately knew exactly what he meant, and where my brother had left the road on his way down the hill from our hunting camp. My response was simply, "When do we leave?"

It was a three hour drive to get back to where we could help Tim. We didn't know what we would do, we simply knew we had to go and help our brother.

We are fiercely loyal to each other. I don't know how it happened. I only know that I share my history with these two men, and to not love them would be a violation of something deep within me, destroying a good deal of who I am.

We are not the same either. We share a common heritage in the family and the neighborhood we grew up in, but each of us are different from the other two.

We have struggled with the differences. In that struggle we have learned we will never be the same, but we will always be brothers. We still compete with each other, and we have now learned to celebrate the abilities and victories of the other.

We are brothers. We have found relationship.

Unconditional

I really like my kids.

Really.

While they were growing up I had the opportunity and great privilege to teach them. I taught them each how to tie their shoes, walk on logs, and drive a stick shift. We went camping, rode bicycles and worked on projects together. I set aside three weekends during several summers to take each one backpacking into an alpine lake in the Cascade Mountains. It was time for just the two of us, and they had my undivided attention. I worked hard to have a relationship with my kids. I have no favorite but treat them each differently, because each one of them is different from the other two.

When they were in their early teens, I sat them down and told them very seriously, "You can move as far away as you possibly can, you can change your name, and you can have surgery to change the way you look, but you will always be my child. Nothing can change that." It was my way of telling them I would always be their dad. I would be there for them, and they could not run away from my love no matter how far they ran.

I am not telling you that my kids were angels growing up. They were kids. They took all of our time and wanted more and they got into things they shouldn't have gotten into.

My wife and I returned home one afternoon after a shopping trip to find some fresh green paint on the garage door. Upon closer inspection we found the green paint was also on the refrigerator in the garage. Then I began to follow the trail of green paint. I found paint on tools, then went out the side door to a rock, the dog house, and then the chocolate lab came up to us wagging his tail with green paint on his head. Our son had found a can of green paint which opened up a world he had not yet explored.

This one was funny, although I didn't laugh too much at the time. I was compelled to be the dad and lecture my son on the proper use of not just green paint, but all color paint.

I would often find their bicycles in the driveway where I parked the car. This always frustrated me. They lied about things, and when they were old enough, they decided they would do what they wanted to do much of the time, in spite of what I wanted them to do.

They were kids.

Recently I received a phone call from my oldest daughter to tell me she had set out simply to prove me wrong. Then she had to admit that I was right, but she did what she did only to prove me wrong. As I did with my parents, my children pulled away to separate from their mother and father in search for their independence. Much of it was unpleasant; some of it was disturbing.

In spite of all they have done, and I wished they wouldn't have, I still like them.

I like them a lot.

They have been the best teachers I could have hoped for in teaching me how to be a parent.

I am learning from them I should not necessarily tell them the answer to a problem they are facing. I'm learning (although I'm not real good at it) it is best in most cases to let them work through it, so they can experience and learn how to process through their decisions.

I once sat next to a man on an airplane. He had been drinking, and he wasn't letting the flying get in the way of his consumption as we flew.

Sometimes with inhibitions lowered and defenses are down, we inadvertently come out of hiding, exposing a part of our hearts.

This was one of those sometimes for this man, and regardless of what I thought or whether or not I was interested in talking, he was going to tell me about his kids. This was not to be a pleasant story. In fact, the more he talked, the more uncomfortable I became. The man had several adult children, and he hated each of them and let me know just how he felt. He proceeded to tell me how worthless they were, and give me the reasons he hated each one. He told me about his daughter who had decided to get her nipples pierced and posed in motorcycles magazines. His son was worthless—couldn't hold a job, and simply wanted his money.

These were his kids.

He hated his kids.

He wanted to continue.

I wanted to find another seat.

And so I did.

I was bewildered that a father could hold so much hostility toward his children, and wondered why he couldn't see their efforts to get his attention and love. I wondered if he had ever noticed that all kids want their father to be proud of them, and they will work to earn it. It seemed he wasn't paying attention to them. He didn't know them. At least that is how it seemed to me. He wasn't asking for answers, and I had none for him, but his hatred toward his children was more than I could bear.

As I considered this man's pain, I had no guarantees that one or all of my kids would not follow the same lifestyle as his children. Regardless of my children's choices, they would still be my children, my offspring. They would hold a place in my heart that no other could threaten or take away from them, simply because they were born to my wife and me; no others could share the journey we have shared as family.

I know there are many, many things they could do to push my acceptance and test my love. And they have.

As I struggled to teach them and give them my best, I asked myself what is really important? What do I want to leave them with? What do they need to navigate the perils of life and discover life on their own?

Is it the color of their hair? My brown-haired son wanted to be blond.

Is it their body piercings or tattoos or lack thereof? (You should know I wanted my girls to wait until they were twenty one or older to get their ears pierced!)

Is it the clothes they wear and how they wear them? Alternative, Goth, or pants down to their knees.

Is their compliance to my ideals and standards what is really important?

Is it really important they follow my counsel for living and behave the way I want them to?

I'm not smart enough to instruct them in all the things they will encounter. I can't possibly see the situations they will face as they grow and work and learn and marry. What I have concluded is there is one thing that matters most to me, one thing that will serve to guide them and direct them.

The one thing that matters most to me is that they have a heart and passion for God.

All else is secondary.

If they can find God and pursue Him, He will lead them and guide them, and who am I to question that?

What's love got to do with it?
Love has everything to do with it.

I don't want the relationship apart from love, if there could be such a thing.

Without love, God becomes indifferent, perhaps a tyrant or a dictator who will press His will onto us, using us or maybe abusing us for His own sadistic pleasure.

We don't matter, and He doesn't care.

Without love, I become a feral child, left to myself and abandoned to the wilderness using whatever I can find to survive.

Without love, death becomes an ally, a possibility to escape the physical suffering and the never ending desire for something I know can never be acquired, for there is no one to give it, and it is nowhere to be found.

Jesus said that He is the way, the truth, and the life.[11] He said that He and His Father are one.[12] Jesus lived life out loud. He displayed love to us in full sight, without fear.

He did it when He showed compassion for the weak and crippled. He did it when He healed the blind and the leper. He did it when He ate with the tax collectors and let the prostitute wash His feet, and said that she, and not the religious elite would be remembered for generations to come. He affirmed the faith of a gentile soldier. He cast out demons. He drove the corruption from the temple. He stood up to religious oppression.

In it all He offered life to any who wanted it.

Love is life. They are synonyms.

The life God created for me, the life He created for us can only be experienced in the context of love. The fullness, the satisfaction, the contentment, and the energy to face all of the chaos and all of the confusion of life, the courage to battle evil, and the energy to engage in the confusion of relationships is all found in the context of love.

Without God, I am left with the inability to receive love and the inability to give it. All I have is my need, and all I can do is put my need and my lust to lyrics and a catchy tune to make it sound acceptable and less offensive.

On this journey to discover life I have learned that God has made us for Himself. He made us to be with Him and He says that He will come and live in me and you and be with us always, in all places.[13] He will never leave us, nor will he turn from us or leave us stranded if we will go to Him to find life.[14]

God has tattooed my name on His heart and His name on mine. We are bound together by the deep roots of family and He claims me as His son.

His love for me as His child is far more committed and fervent than the love I have for my children.

He is not unhappy with me.

He is proud of me, and I do not have to try and earn His love.

He appreciates my gratitude and loves to love me.

As for my wife, we still have trouble communicating and still misunderstand each other. But over the years our love has grown from our commitment to each other. We fit together well, and I can't imagine life without her. She has taught me a good deal about life and love, and I am looking forward to growing old with her.

She has taught me that love does not withdraw. It stays engaged, even when damaged or painful. Love costs a great deal. Just look at the price God paid in loving us.

Relationship is still a mystery to me. What has love got to do with it?

Everything. Love is the stuff of relationship, the very fabric of the connection, the bond of family; it is the divine link to God.

To not love God is the greatest sin I could ever commit.

It is more than rejecting the generosity and grace of the only One I can trust. It is a rejection of who I am and how I was made. To not love is to curse Him as Creator Father and reject all He has attempted to give me and provide for me.

My sin is much more than simply disobedience; it is that I reject God's assistance to find the life I want. I want to find it on my own. I want to be separate, to do it myself, my way. And then, filled with ingratitude and pride, I want to tell God that I am a good person because of all of the good things that I've done, and that He should give me what I want and let me make a wonderful home in a place away from Him.

Would you force someone to live with you who didn't want to be with you, or would you let them choose to live separate, away from you?

Who do you love?
The question was no accident. After His resurrection and after Peter's denial, it was no accident that Jesus asked Peter a simple question.

"Peter, do you love me?" [15]

You might remember the story where a few days earlier Peter had boasted with great confidence that even though all the

others might betray Jesus, he certainly would not. Not him.
No way. [16] Yet when the time came Peter could not admit to
a little servant girl that he was a friend of Jesus. [17]

So much for Peter's fearless courage.

And Jesus came to Peter and asked him, "Do you love me?"

"Greater love has no one than this, that one lay down his life
for his friends." [18]

Jesus had laid His life down for His friends. He demonstrated
His love when He asked the young man to follow Him, to be
one of His twelve. He demonstrated His love in His teaching
and sharing His meals, and in the daily routines of walking,
talking, and laughing with Peter and the others.

Peter was there. He saw and experienced Jesus' love first
hand. And then Peter witnessed Jesus literally lay down His
life. Peter witnessed the act.

Now Jesus simply wanted to know if Peter loved Him.

To Peter's credit, when He discovered it was Jesus on the
shore calling to them, he jumped in the water and swam
ashore.

He went to Jesus with urgency.

The greatest sin we can commit is not to respond with love to
a God who loves us enough to die for us that we might have
life.

I simply don't know how to love. And this is the crux of my sin.

I must go to Him.

Twelve

I Think I Can Dance

"Love is letting go of fear"—Gerald G. Jampolsky

Who do you trust?

My family celebrates Christmas at least twice each year. Call us masochists if you like, but we have a day or weekend after Christmas when all of my extended family gather to eat a big meal, play, and let the kids open the gifts from grandma and grandpa.

We call it the McCoy Christmas. It is not about gifts. It is simply about family and hanging out.

It is a lot of work to get five families scheduled on a day or weekend. It is one more thing in the midst of an already busy season that demands preparation and time—time that is often very difficult to find. It is stressful at times, and the preparation is demanding. It adds more tension to life that I would rather avoid, tension from misunderstandings, from trying to coordinate with all of the extended family, and the chaos of so many people trying to live together for even a day or two. Sometimes it is just messy.

That is what we call the McCoy family Christmas. It is all of the confusion you would expect in a family of twenty-five people with different needs, appetites, and desires for what the weekend will be or should be.

This year we held the event at my brother and sister-in-law's home. After the meal, as all of us sat around wondering what to do next, my niece put a CD on by Josh Turner and played a song he wrote to his wife called "Your Man." Josh has a mellow and deep baritone voice, and the song starts with his low voice singing to his wife, "Baby lock the door and turn the lights down low." It is a fun song about the seductive beauty of the relationship given to a man and wife. My niece decided my brothers and I should sing it to our wives along with the CD.

My brothers did not choose choir in school, and we are not given to sing for the family. We play in front of them, and we play with them, but we don't sing. We'll shoot hoops, hit golf balls, sled down steep hills, and throw things, but we don't sing. Unless you happen to find us in church following along with the other hundred or so people in a chorus, we don't sing.

It's simply not something we do.

I really like Josh Turner, and I really like the song. For some reason beyond my ability to explain to you, I took the bait and stood up to sing to my wife. I also invited her to dance with me, not that I know how to dance, mind you, but it all seemed reasonable at the time, and I was met with little or no resistance from myself as I engaged in the exhibition.

As I sang to my wife and danced around the floor (at least it was my attempt to dance), I overheard my oldest daughter saying, "two years ago dad would have never danced or sang!" And she was right. But right then, in that time and place, it simply didn't matter. I was enjoying myself, my wife, and the freedom to dance, play, and sing, and simply look silly.

For me it was a moment to live life out loud. It simply didn't matter to me what anyone thought.

It didn't matter if I looked stupid or silly.

It simply didn't matter.

It was quite a rare experience for me. I am not claiming that dancing in front of your family is all that big of a deal. They might laugh at me and make fun of me a bit, but they are family. They really can't get rid of me. But this was, for a few moments, stepping out from behind my protective cover. Somehow I had the courage to risk the exposure and found there a sense of freedom I had not known for a long, long time, possibly since I was a very young boy.

As I try to manage the chaos of my everyday life, it is my nature to avoid anything that might make me feel stupid or silly, or anything I think someone else would think me stupid or silly. What I have to live with when I choose living with so much self-protection is a suffocation of the life that I want, suffocation from the fear of exposure and ridicule.

I am coming to the conclusion the life I want is not going to be found in my self-protection. The safety and security I have worked so hard at trying to manage for so many years does not allow life to breath until I am willing to get up and dance, regardless of what anyone else thinks of me. I am learning that God has entered into the chaos that I call life, and His main goal is not to make life more orderly or safer for me. His main task is to help me trust Him in the chaos, so that I can discover the life I am looking for in the midst of my confusion and life's chaos.

God somehow has interrupted this journey of mine and introduced Himself. In ways I can barely understand, let alone fully explain, He has bent down and hugged me. Over and over again He has said He loves me. And as the chaos overwhelms me, and my confusion befuddles me, I am reduced to facing the fact that God is God, and I am not, that somehow He is in charge of the big and little things that happen to me, and that the path to find life is to follow His lead through the confusion.

I must trust Him.

No. I don't believe He causes the bad things to happen to us, yet bad things do happen. The God I read about is bigger than any or all of those things that happen to me. So when the Bible says that "all things" will work together for good it means *all things*, not some things and not most things but *all things*.

That means to me that God is bigger than *all things*.

It is much easier for me to *say* I believe, that I trust God with all things, than it is for me to *act* as if I believe that all things are working out and He is in charge.

Sometimes I am simply too afraid to stand up and dance. Sometimes the fear of what I think people are thinking or what they might think about me is greater than I can overcome. Sometimes I am simply afraid of what might happen.

And so I hold back. I keep to myself. I need to protect what I have, who I am.

Sometimes when I remember that God likes me, when I remember that He has stepped into my life to hug me, I am not so afraid anymore.

Then is when it is easier to dance.

I don't always dance and I don't always remember, but when I do, it is easier to take the risk.

What am I doing?
I am sitting here at my computer trying to arrange my thoughts into a logical order. I hope I am able to arrange them in such a way that someone will be able to relate to them and find some benefit.

Can we talk? Can I be really honest with you?

This is scaring me to death.

This is an idea that began about ten years ago. Over the years there has been a fragile confidence that has helped me to get to this point in the process. Many times I have walked away from this effort, only to return to it a few months or years later. At one point I tried to dismiss it completely, to rid myself of the hassle.

I simply have not been able to divorce myself from it.

He wouldn't let me.

A few years ago I wrestled through two weeks of sleepless nights before I gave in and agreed to continue. I have been able to sleep since then, but frankly the process has been challenging and very difficult for me. I have no idea if anyone will ever read this, let alone find any benefit from my effort.

But it is not the difficulty that has held me back. Nor is it wondering if anyone will find any benefit from the many years and the effort I've spent.

What frightens me is the exposure.

It took six years of effort before I could admit out loud that I was writing to anyone else, and then I started with only the safest people I know.

Admitting to someone else that I was writing a book opens me up to feelings I do not fully understand. It is similar to the insecurity I felt when I lined up at the starting line for my first marathon. Standing there at the starting line, dressed up in my running gear, I was announcing to the world my intension to run for 26.2 miles.

I don't think the world cared.

I suppose all of these feelings of insecurity come from within me. All of the uncertainty I sense is simply from my self-talk.

Can I really do this?

No one should ever run for 26.2 miles!

What if I get to twenty miles and can't go any further? I've never done this before.

And now I am attempting to write a book.

Do we really need another book?

Probably not.

I think there are many people who have said or are saying what I am trying to say much better than I can. You should read their books. It would probably make more sense to you than mine.

But this is my story.

This is my attempt to say the things that I have been learning through the stories God has given me.

No one else has been given these stories.

No one else can tell them the way I tell them.

No one else has lived these stories in this place and time.

Perhaps there is someone that can relate to them. Perhaps my kids will enjoy them.

But the exposure is still terrifying at times. The choice I am left with is whether or not I will let the fear drive me. There is so much that I do from fear. Trying to protect myself, trying to avoid getting hurt, trying to keep my life together, afraid that it is coming apart at the seams.

It is all defensive.

Then I read that Jesus said, "Whoever desires to save his life will lose it, but whoever loses his life for My sake will find it." [19]

I think He is talking about me, attempting to protect my life, to keep it safe, to manage it well, to save it. That is where fear takes me. Fear keeps me hidden. I take no risks. I keep my place and stay in line. There is comfort and security in my place, hidden in the crowd.

Not all fear is bad, mind you. The Bible says that the fear of God is the beginning of wisdom. So there is a good fear that leads me to God, the part of fear that leads to wisdom.

I told you of the sleepless nights and that God would not let me alone until I agreed to do this. That is a fear of God, born of respect and where submission finds its feet. Perhaps I am finding a proper fear of God that is greater than my fear of exposure.

The kind of fear I don't want is the crippling, debilitating fear that does not allow me to take any risk, the suffocating fear that keeps me in hiding. It is the kind of fear that forfeits my God-given responsibility for me, and tries to make someone else responsible for me, rewarding me with the ability to complain and blame others for my problems and difficulties. It is the fear of exposure, the kind of fear that urges me to walk away from this computer.

That is the fear that suffocates the life I want to live. It is the fear I don't want to live with.

I can't tell you how many times I have been afraid as I boarded a plane for a business trip, or as I prepared to leave on a weekend camping trip or began an effort to organize an event. The fear wells up within me asking, what are you doing?

Sometimes I feel stupid, insignificant, and foolish for even thinking of making the effort.

Yet somehow I am pressed forward.

Just as I am now.

Life is not found in the fear. I must not succumb to the apprehension. I must find the courage to take the risk and see what happens, even if nothing happens, and no one ever knows.

You see, the writing is for you, but the effort I am putting forth is for me. It is my battle against my fear. It is my search to find life.

In a very real way, it is dying to the self in me that seeks to protect me and keep me safe, so that I might find the life that is promised to me.

The Chicken Little syndrome

Listening to talk radio or the nightly news or reading the headlines does not help to settle my fear. Much of the public conversation is all about fear. There is such a steady offering of fear that sometimes it leaves me with the impression they are peddling fear as a drug.

I listened to a politician speaking to a committee of politicians about how my children and grandchildren are facing certain catastrophe, the real end of the world if we do not address the growing epidemic of global warming. They say in the last 150 years of the world the earth's average temperature has increased one degree Fahrenheit.

Fear.

Somehow the earth and the elements that influence the cycles of nature are out of control and need our attention. We are now responsible for the problem, and they need to increase our taxes in order to manage the problem. Then we can feel safer that their efforts will save us and our children from certain disaster.

How did the Earth ever survive to this point in history?

Am I being sarcastic? Absolutely.

I remember in grade school they told us we were in jeopardy of a new ice age. That the Earth could change its polar caps, and the ice would form over the populated areas causing great catastrophe to life as we know it. Now, a few years later it is Global Warming.

Fear.

Maybe they feel guilty? Whatever the motivation, for some reason they feel responsible to take care of us and save the world.

I am not against conservation and stewardship. I am against using fear to manipulate me or the public opinion. I am against the messages blaming me for global warming or holding me responsible for the poverty in India.

Guilt and fear are great motivators. I have enough of my own without others piling on, thank you very much!

In the opening scene of the movie, *The Village*, the camera pans a grave site memorial for a seven- year-old boy with the dates 1890-1897 chiseled on the tombstone. The residents live in a small, isolated town, surrounded by a perimeter fence. They dress in subdued colors so as to not attract the wrath of the feared creatures of the forest.

But it was all a hoax created by the town leaders who had suffered personal tragedy in the crowded twentieth century. They had become a support group and had retreated to the

wooded estate of a wealthy doctor. They used fear to manage
and control their children in an effort to keep them in the
small town, protecting them from the danger of crowded
cities and the chaos and confusion of life.

We have become so familiar with fear that it seems a
reasonable tool of manipulation—a reasonable tool that we
use against others when it is expedient, and often we don't
object when others use it against us.

I hope you dance

A few years ago Lee Ann Womack released the song, "I Hope
You Dance." It is a song I still enjoy listening to. It is a dream
and a wish about life and living, about keeping the desire for
the search and the hunger for life. It is a song filled with
encouragement to face the fear and never settle for less, but
"when you get the choice to sit it out or dance, I hope you
dance."

I don't expect we'd need encouragement to live life if it were
easy.

It wouldn't mean anything if risking and pursuing life were
normal for us—if it were how we lived each day.

But it's not how we live.

That is why we need the encouragement to take the risk and
live.

I find fear reasoning with me in almost every endeavor I
undertake. My God-given desires and dreams often if not

always stir up fear within me. The desires and dreams are simply dangerous and risky. The fear within me demands that the desires and dreams of my heart be managed. The fear demands that I protect, stay safe, move with caution, retreat and withdraw. Dreams are fine as long as they are reasonable. Desires can be tolerated as long as they are feeble. They must be kept small, manageable, not too threatening; otherwise ...

... they are simply too dangerous.

I am captive, prisoner, as they say, to my fear and its demands on me.

My fear is willing to build a wall of isolation to protect me, sometimes pushing me, sometimes holding me back, constantly looking for danger, and assessing the risk of my actions and reactions. Fear has become my guide.

Fear, in all of its well meaning efforts to protect me, cannot give me life. It leaves me thirsty, cut off and isolated from the life I want to live.

Jesus told a story of a man who bought and sold pearls for a living.[20] I expect as he worked in the trade he learned much about the quality and value of pearls. I expect he made some poor decisions and some good ones as he managed his inventory of pearls. In the process he learned how to tell the good pearls from the bad and the real good ones from the average pearls.

Then the pearl merchant found a pearl that caught his eye. It was the most spectacular pearl he had ever seen. Larger than any other with a dazzling display of color and quality greater than any of the really good pearls he had ever bought or sold.

And he sold all that he had, so he could buy this one pearl.

The merchant risks everything to buy the one pearl. When it says he sold all that he had, does that mean everything?

His business?

His car?

His house?

I suspect he didn't consider it to be a great risk. He knew pearls. He knew the value of this one was worth it all. It was no blind leap for him. His love for pearls had taught him all about their worth. He may have been afraid of losing the pearl or of someone stealing the pearl or of the market dropping and the pearl losing its value—but he was not afraid of selling all he had to obtain the pearl.

What does he do with the pearl when he gets it?

Does he put it away where no one can see it?

Does he protect it?

Does he share the beauty with others?

How does he make his living now?

Jesus doesn't tell us more about the merchant. It is a simple parable meant to illustrate a point. The point is that life in the kingdom of heaven is like that great pearl. It is worth all that we have and all we own. It should be so obvious to us in our search for life that the promise overcomes the hesitation; the great love given us overcomes our fear.

Thirteen

Grace is Much Bigger Than I Thought it Was

"I know now, Lord, why you utter no answer. You are yourself the answer. Before your face questions die away."—CS Lewis

I once was blind, but now I see

A parole officer I knew shared an experience with me about a phone call she had received from a distraught young man. He was reporting his wife's parole violation in a desperate attempt to rescue his young bride. My friend, the parole officer, told me the young man's wife had been recently arrested for drug abuse, and the courts had assigned the young woman's case to her.

The distraught husband led the police to a dingy one room apartment where they found his young wife in a semi comatose stupor, oblivious to all of the commotion of the arresting officers, lying naked on the bed in the room.

The first course of action for the officers was the arrest of the man found in the room with her, first for drug possession, and then for his outstanding warrants. Once he was apprehended they were able to turn their attention to the young woman. As they did, her husband turned to my friend with a plea for permission to cover his bride's shame. My friend agreed, and watched in awe as he, with great care and compassion, covered his bride in an effort to restore some of her dignity in preparation for her trip to jail.

My friend, as she shared the story with me, told me that as she watched the young man, she heard within her, a gentle voice say, *"That is what I have done for you."*

From the beginning I had listened to my friend's story with sincere interest in her and her work. I was not expecting the ending, and it had left me speechless, stunned from the imagery and the truth it held. I was not expecting to hear such a vivid illustration of love and life from such a broken and discarded part of our world. For my friend, the dirty apartment had been transformed into a holy place as God exposed Himself for a moment, allowing both her and now me to see into His heart and the great compassion He has for us.

I suppose that what stunned me the most was God showing up in such a dirty place. Maybe my disbelief is because of my pride or perhaps simply my arrogance. I thought God kept Himself apart from the dirty places. I thought God separated Himself from the rebellious, those who choose sin, and the people that so willingly turned their backs on Him. I know

God cares for all people. I know He paid a great price to cover the sin and dirt of all people, but aren't we supposed to be separated from the bad stuff we seem to enjoy in order to meet Him? Aren't there some rules we are supposed to follow to please Him?

I always understood these rules to be the requirements of learning to follow and please God. People who choose to live in the world of drugs, sex and alcohol simply choose to live outside of the world where I thought God would show up. At least He wouldn't show up in a way that I would want to meet Him. If God were to show up and find me in the dirty places of life I would expect that He would be very angry that I had broken His rules.

Isn't that the way it works?

My friend's story haunted me. I imagined myself to be the young man and the mixed feelings of betrayal and love. What was he feeling as he discovered his wife in such a state? He had found her naked, what she had promised to give only to him was exposed to the world after she had given it to another man. He had found her intoxicated, unaware of his very presence after ingesting enough drugs and alcohol to sedate her common sense.

How could he still love her?

How could his heart endure the betrayal?

What compelled him to bear her shame and stand in the midst of a crowded room and claim her as his wife and cover her?

I am not claiming to understand this picture I was given. I am not telling you I comprehend grace and all that it means. This thing that God calls grace is much bigger and more dangerous than I ever imagined. I am only beginning to understand that grace has more depth to it, that it reaches freely into more places than I have ever thought possible.

It is changing my view of God.

My view of God began to take shape in a small community church in a small backwoods town. For many years I attended simply because I had no choice. For the most part, I enjoyed my childhood there. As I moved into my teenage years and I began to form my own questions, I had an increasing dissatisfaction with the answers they offered. At seventeen I took my questions and moved away to see if I could discover on my own more satisfying answers in my journey to discover life. After a few years of experience and making a little progress with my questions, I returned home and to the little church when I was twenty-one.

The church was so small that in many ways we were our own small group. It was here in this context that many of my ideas and images of Christianity were formed. Somehow in the midst of the Sunday School classes and potlucks, I had collected and assembled my mental list of things that one must do in order to be a Christian. This list contained both the things that would disqualify one from being a Christian and the list of things that a Christian did. This list of rules became my personal list of qualifications and disqualifications of a "true Christian"

As you already know, the process of learning means that my list was not a firm, fixed list, but rather a dynamic list that I was amending as I discovered more about what God expects from us and the rules He has given us to live by. At one point in my journey, I remember thinking I should work through the New Testament, particularly the letters Paul wrote with instructions to the new believers, so I could make a more complete and accurate list of what I should do and what I should not do.

I really wanted to get it right.

For some reason, possibly my lack of commitment and dedication, I never made the list of the rules.

Gradually, over many years, the stories in the Bible became more than the flannel board narratives with heroes that conquered giants and armies that I had learned about as a young boy. I began to see the humanity of the heroes and the ancient world they lived in began to seem more like the world I lived in. I also began to notice that God did not abandon the people when they chose to break His rules. I began to notice that many of the places His people chose to run to looked more and more like a little dingy one room apartment.

Then I began to notice how God sought them out and covered their nakedness.

As I began to see better, my list of how a Christian should look and behave began to come apart.

I did not understand how God could accept—no, I did not understand how God could love the people He would find in the dingy one room apartments of the world.

Didn't He make the rules?

Aren't we supposed to follow these rules to please Him?

Perspective

Someone told me a story of a motorist driving his brand new car along the highway, enjoying the day and the winding road as the pavement led him through the hills and valleys. Feeling very satisfied with the performance of the new car, he noticed ahead on the side of the road a young boy standing next to the guard rail looking at him as he approached.

The boy's eyes were fixed on the approaching car. It didn't seem out of the ordinary to see a young boy on the side of the road. The kids used the road to travel back and forth alongside the motorists, but it seemed a little odd the way the boy was standing. As the motorist approached in his new car the boy reached down to pick up something and raised his arm as if to throw it. Then, sure enough, he threw it right at the new car.

A rock.

I once had a kid throw a tennis ball at my car as I drove by. I stopped and chased him into his house. This motorist reacted the same way I did.

He jammed on the brakes, stopping his car a short distance beyond the delinquent. Jumping out of the car to begin the chase with the intent of bringing the boy to justice for the insult and damage to his new car, he began to close the gap between him and the offender. The boy made no attempt to flee. In fact, to the surprise of the motorist he held his position alongside the barrier. He expected the boy to run.

The boy didn't. For some reason, the he just stood there, waiting.

Undeterred, he ran up to the boy, but before he could vent his anger, the boy blurted out, "Mister, please call the ambulance." The motorist's eyes began to notice a twisted pile of bicycle halfway down the hill from the boy.

"My friend crashed on his bike, and I can't wake him up." The man's eyes then found the motionless boy at the bottom of the hill.

"Please call 911."

Perspective.

I do not have the ability to view life from another person's vantage point. I can't understand what motivates another person to do what they do or think what they think.

I simply do not understand. Much of what I see people do makes little or no sense to me.

Sometimes when I take the time to see it or hear it from their perspective I can understand a little better.

In my search for life, to feel and to live the life that I believe I was meant to live, I have broken many rules, some of my own rules and many of God's rules. I have sampled many of the offerings that were appealing to me. I have made many attempts to feel life and to anesthetize the wounds and pain of my failures.

If I would have looked around, if I could have sobered up to see and pay attention to where I had taken refuge, I think I could have seen the dirty walls of the dingy one room apartment.

If I had been able to look up, I would have seen a young Jewish Rabbi waiting to cover my shame with His own garments.

That is the grace I am coming to know.

A grace that moves beyond my ideas of right and wrong, of acceptable and unacceptable and moves into the dirty dingy apartments of life to cover the shame of people. It is very difficult for me to see that grace is meant for the dirty one room apartments of the world. It is even harder for me to recognize that I am often the one lying naked on the bed in the dingy apartment.

I am not quite sure I am convinced yet, but I am finding that to know grace, I must begin with understanding that grace is personal. Grace is my need. As it becomes personal I am able to know how grace meets my need and then I find I have more compassion to give others as they search for life, struggling with their own demons along the way.

We are desperate to find life as God meant for us to live. Life as God designed it for you and me. And so we resort to doing whatever we think will help us find that life. If I believe living by the rules that God has given us, the rules that I have learned from learning and studying His Word, if I believe conformance to these rules is my access to grace, then my understanding and application of grace becomes how I understand and apply the rules. I can only extend grace to you when you use the same rules that I use to search with, and only when your effort to find life breaks the same rules that I break. Then it won't bother me that you use the same hiding places or methods to deaden the pain.

I understand and can justify efforts and failures that are similar to mine. And that becomes the extent of the grace I can offer you.

The problem is presented when you have learned different rules than the ones I have learned and live by. I don't understand when you break my rules or why you would think that your rules would be superior to the ones I have chosen to live with. Because I don't understand the rules you choose and why you think them important, I find it easy to condemn you for the hiding places that you choose to use.

I can't understand why you are unable to understand grace the way I understand it. I don't know why you cannot understand the rules as I do and why you can't see the importance of not offending God in the same way that I understand Him to be offended.

And so I view the world as a dirty one room apartment, and I see many people choosing to live there, but am unable to see that I am only looking out the window of my own dirty one room apartment, believing my dirt to be cleaner than everyone else's.

I am concluding that my understanding of grace has been too small. In fact, you could argue that it hasn't been grace at all.

Maybe it hasn't.

As I realize that I am the one that has been found naked and began to see through my own haze the face of the One who covers me, then is when I begin to perceive a grace much bigger than I have ever imagined. When I understand my own search for life has brought me to this place, and that you too are searching for life, just as I am, that your efforts are in fact an attempt to satisfy the longing that God has placed in your heart, when I understand that we are both searching and stumbling, I find I can begin to share with you the same compassion that He showed me.

Perhaps I am beginning to understand grace.

Grace is not blind

There is a good deal of difficulty in what I am trying to communicate. This is not easy, as I can't say I fully understand how comprehensive grace really is. What I do see is a grace that reaches into the filthy and dirty apartments of the world to the people who have wanted nothing to do with God or goodness or church, and that grace covers them. A grace that changes people's hearts and offers them life, full, rich, and abundant. It is a grace big enough to cover me and you.

Not because we have earned it.

But simply because He loves us.

Don't misunderstand; grace doesn't pretend that we have done nothing wrong. This is a grace that has clearly seen the wrong and has dealt with it, enduring the pain, the suffering, and the penalty of the misbehavior, disobedience, and transgression that you and I have committed.

This is a grace that sends us to rehab and stays engaged with us as we suffer through the withdrawals and relapses. It is a grace that pursues us when we hide, looking to find some relief from the chaos by returning to our dirty apartment.

It is also a grace that respects us, sometimes allowing us to wallow in the dirt and eat the filth of our choices. It waits with longing for us to return, while giving us the freedom to live in the dirt.

Truth and love are companions of grace.

To live in God's grace we must face the truth about ourselves, coming to terms with who we really are, and learn to love by first receiving the love He gives us and then, in return offering the same to others.

Grace is forgiveness and restoration. Grace is the covering for my offense. Grace cleans up the mess I made, but it does not overlook the fact that I made the mess. When grace covers my mess it does not look the other way as if it never happened, hoping it will not happen again or excusing the offense. Grace is strong enough to endure the pain, gentle enough to comfort, and courageous enough to lead us with truth and wisdom.

Nathan, the prophet, extended grace to the most powerful man in the land, the king. He told him a story of a man and his pet lamb—a poor man who purchased this one lamb that he loved and cared for. Then his wealthy neighbor, who is described to own flocks and herds, stole the lamb, because he was unwilling to take an animal from his own to feed a traveler who happened by and was staying with him for an evening.

The king became very angry and vowed to administer justice to the selfish and inconsiderate man who would take a poor man's sheep and kill it to save his own possessions.

Then Nathan looked at the king and said, "You are that man." [21]

It was the king, already having many wives of his own, who had taken another man's wife, and slept with her. When he discovered that she was pregnant, he had the man killed to cover his deed.

Nathan told the king the truth. He told the truth to the king, all of his advisors, and all of the guards, and whoever else happened to be in the king's chambers at the time.

I don't believe I would have done that.

Some of those standing in the room were well aware of the king's crimes. Some of them had helped make the arrangements. Some had witnessed them from a distance, and I suspect others would have heard through the grapevine. No one had the courage to correct the king.

I don't believe I would have had the courage to face the man that could have me killed by a wave of his hand and tell him a story to expose him, ruining his reputation and uncovering the sin he had worked so hard to hide.

But Nathan did.

Grace looks the transgression in the eye and calls it what it is. It is not an attempt to humiliate or demean or stand over the other person gloating, because it was them and not you.

Grace sees the evil. It does not simply overlook it. Grace seeks to rehabilitate. Grace requires responsibility. Grace enters the dirty room and in love covers to offer redemption and rehabilitation.

Grace does not bring judgmental condescension.

It is my own judgmental condescension that confirms I still have much to learn about grace. Jesus said we would be judged by the measure we use to judge others. I used to think He meant He would measure me by the same measure that I would use when I judged others. That the same standards that I used to determine the merit of your behavior, good or bad, would be the measure to determine the merits of my behavior.

I no longer think that is what Jesus meant.

I am coming to see that I am judged by the same measure I use to judge another person, but I am the one who holds me to that measure. If I have decided that saying a certain word is wrong or that a certain behavior is immoral, and you are less of a Christian when you use that word or behave in that way, I will think the same of myself when I use the word or behave in that way.

If I believe perfect church attendance is a noble deed that all Christians should attain then I will hold myself to that standard, priding myself on my accomplishments and viewing all who miss church as living a lower standard of Christianity. I will then condemn myself if I don't keep up my record of perfect church attendance.

The standard that I use to decide the merits of everyone else is what I use to determine my own merits. It is the standard that will accuse me. It is the standard that I cannot live up to, and it is often the genesis for my unreasonable anger.

I may seem hard on how I judge others, but in reality I am much harder on myself.

If I have little grace for you it is because I have little grace for myself. The grace I live by is only big enough to meet the rules I have established for myself to live by and with. It is only big enough to cover the little transgressions I may commit, but it could never reach into a dirty little apartment.

God's grace is much bigger than I ever imagined it to be, and I believe it is much bigger than I am able to describe to you here.

It is as big as God is.

As my friend would say, it is how He rolls.

Fourteen

How Should We Then Live

The glory and joy of life is not found in perfection but in the chaos and confusion of living.

Just to make you proud

I moved away from home when I was seventeen. After living in two other states for three years, I moved back to live with my parents. In the course of the year that followed I found a job, met my wife, and began my life of responsibility and independence. It was during that year of transition I remember standing in front of the garage talking with my dad, while the morning sun was breaking through the trees. I don't recall the all of the details of the conversation, but I do remember the three years away from home had led me to a much deeper appreciation of my father. I had found a deep gratitude for not only what he taught me and how he had prepared me, but for the man he was.

Before I tell you about how our conversation ended, you should know my dad was not a man who expressed a great deal of affection. He was very easy going and pleasant, while at the same time very guarded with his emotions. I don't remember many great displays of affection to my mother, and he never planned a party or a celebration to my knowledge. His idea of a good time was going camping and having a beer with a friend while sitting around the campfire "shooting the breeze." He wasn't cold or hard or distant. He was approachable, friendly, and loved to laugh. I never met anyone who didn't like my dad. It wasn't that he had no emotion or affection; he simply didn't freely express them.

As was his way, I never heard my dad tell me he loved me. He didn't tell my siblings either, and I don't remember ever hearing him tell Mom that he loved her. It simply wasn't necessary. He displayed it to us in the way he lived with us.

In a conversation about dad with one of my brothers, I raised the question of whether Dad had ever said that he loved him. His reply was without hesitation. "Of course not! He didn't have to!"

It was an unspoken truth for Dad. We knew he loved us by how he treated us and the consideration he gave us. He had taken us camping most weekends of every summer. He taught us about the woods, how to fish and hunt, how to build a fire, how to swim a river, and how to determine whether the mountain water was okay to drink. He taught us how to work and how to play. We didn't talk about love much; it was simply demonstrated in the way he lived his life—by how he had included us into the most important parts of who he was.

So it was I found myself early in my adult journey, in front of our garage as the sun came up, stumbling over the words to express my appreciation for what this man had provided me during my years of childhood and feeling rather awkward about my efforts. I had not learned to express my feelings from Dad, so this was unfamiliar territory for me.

Looking back at that moment, I suppose a little head nod and a slight smile may have been all that my dad thought was needed. After all, that seemed to be his method of communicating approval and affection. But a simple head nod and smile was not sufficient for me on this day. I needed to put words to the feelings within me. I had said it the best way I knew how, and then to let him know that I loved him too, I took a step closer to my dad, wrapped my arms around him and gave him a big hug.

What I remember from that moment is my dad didn't know what to do, so he just stood there and took it like a man. His arms did not reciprocate, but neither did he withdraw from my embrace.

I remember the moment very clearly.

I would describe the experience very much like hugging a telephone pole. I stepped back and looked my dad in the eyes and said, "Dad, I just want to make you proud."

He didn't say anything. I don't think he knew what to say. Thinking back, he may have given me his smile and head nod to let me know he understood what I had said.

Then the conversation was over.

He never said what he thought of my hug, and he never told me whether he was proud of me or not. I suppose it was the way my dad managed the demons in his own life, he simply didn't talk about that kind of thing. A few years later my dad died of cancer. That was 1981.

I am much older now. I have now reached an age that my dad never reached. Older, and I think a little wiser than I was then, I still want to make my dad proud.

I have shared that story with many men. Most of the responses I have received have been a head nod in agreement, an affirmation of what they know in their own heart. They also still want to make their dad proud.

Kids want to make their dads proud of them, even fifty-year-old kids.

My dad was part of my inheritance. The story I am living today and all my dad was to me, I count as an incredible gift. I want to acknowledge that not all dads have left their children with good memories. Some dads have been abusive, and some absent. Yet it seems even when fathers have set poor examples, leaving only pain and abuse as a memory, their kids still seem to look for a father's approval. Looking for my father's approval is the reason I still do some of the things I do. I want to make Dad proud of me, even though I know he's gone.

This common thread in the hearts of children is part of our design. It is how we are made, to gain the approval of our fathers, to somehow make them proud of us.

Years after that morning in front of the garage, I have kids of my own. In fact, my son and his wife gave me the gift of being called "Grandpa." I am pretty amazed at the experience. Frankly, the whole thing caught me a bit off guard. I suppose it has something to do with my kid having a kid of his own.

When my granddaughter was born she didn't do very much. At four months she didn't do much of anything, good or bad. I remember her learning to laugh and recognize her mom and dad. She would sometimes give me the impression she enjoyed my company but I don't think she really knew who I was.

None-the-less I found myself exceptionally fond of this little girl. I loved to hold her and comfort her. It didn't matter to me if she spit up or was fussy; I simply enjoyed her. As I sat with her in my arms, enjoying her company, it dawned on me that this must be similar to how God feels. He simply enjoys me. Not because of what I do or how obedient I am or how pure I try to make myself, but just because I am His.

I can't do much of anything to make myself any better than I am. I have tried really hard, and I simply do not have the ability. It doesn't seem to matter to Him that I fuss and fret, busying myself with all that I believe to be so critical and so important. What matters most to Him is that I come to Him.

He simply wants to enjoy me.

It is what He wants of each of us. He wants us to come to Him so He can enjoy us and we in turn can enjoy Him.

My good friend Ray had told me many times as he raised his two girls that he wasn't raising children, he was raising people whom he could enjoy spending time with. There is no greater gift that I can receive from my children than that they enjoy spending time with me. All it takes is a quick phone call, a casual meal, or a camping trip where we can talk and laugh and work through the chaos and confusion of life together— simply enjoying each other's company on this journey of life.

Frankly, it is easier for me to believe that God feels that way about you. It is hard for me to believe that God feels that way about me. There are probably a number of reasons, but I just find it difficult to think that He isn't stern and stiff, looking at me with suspicion, waiting for my inevitable misdeed.

Does He really like me? Really?

Chaos and confusion

My life has been filled with confusion and defined by chaos. Choices that seem right at the time rarely turn out the way I intend. The consequences of my choice are compounded by a seemingly endless sequence of events that serve only to keep me off balance. The chaos seems to be unending, the confusion a constant companion. As hard as I try to eliminate them or distance myself from them, they seem to be the base elements of my life.

From simple observation and conversation, I don't think my life is much different than anyone else's. The struggle to order and arrange life, to tame the chaos and make sense of the confusion seems to be simply the way things are. It is the way of life. Some try harder than others to organize and manage the chaos.

In my quest to replace the chaos and confusion with beauty and glory I have tried to discover how I was created to live. Wishing I could spend more time with beauty and glory I discovered that my companions, chaos and confusion have been leading me to a beauty beyond what I could have imagined, and a glory far bigger than my small life can contain. I am amazed to think that without chaos and confusion, I would have never experienced the glimpses of beauty and glory.

It was my inability to order and manage my life that forced me to look to someone else for help. I simply couldn't do enough, or work hard enough to manage my life. My inability to subdue the chaos, or manage my confusion or conquer my sin forced me to look to Him.

That was always the point wasn't it?

It was when I went to Him that I discovered He loves me, far bigger, much wider, and so much deeper than I ever imagined.

The beauty is overwhelming.

The glory stunning.

This is what I am searching for. I *am* feeling alive. This is *life*.

Life is living in the presence and glory of One who is bigger than the chaos, One whom I can trust with my confusion, and One who has suffered the pain and is able to bring much beauty out of what appears to be such a mess.

I am discovering *life*.

Come to the party

It took me a long time to see it. I spent most of my time trying to learn proper teaching and theology, the correct and proper approach to living the life as God designed it. I spent so much time trying to get it right that I just didn't see it.

God invites us to party.

Really.

Right there in the middle of all the instructions God was giving His people on how to live, there is a list of the parties He wanted His people to throw. He wanted the people to set aside time, to stop working and celebrate.

Sometimes for days at a time.

I grew up with an image of God as being real serious. He was busy putting things back to the order that He meant for them when He created everything, and figuring out who was going to be punished for His coming day of judgment. I grew up understanding that His rules were very, very important, and if I was to be on His good side then I must pay attention to His rules.

He didn't seem all that friendly to me. It seemed that he was busy about His business with a stern face, disappointed at how things turned out, and somber about how things were progressing. How could anyone so serious and strict be interested in parties?

Yet there they are, right alongside all of the rules. Instructions to cease all work and throw a party.

Gather together.

Celebrate.

Eat.

Drink.

Remember.

The first miracle Jesus performed was at a wedding party. [22] It was a big deal to run out of wine at a wedding party. It must have been a big party to need an additional one hundred-fifty or so gallons of wine, and to have a "master of the party."

This partying simply does not fit into my image of God.

Big parties.

Several hundred gallons of wine.

The only logical conclusion is that my image of God must be twisted and warped.

Why so many parties? Why so much frivolous activity with nothing to show for it but the empty wine glasses, dirty plates and leftover food?

Sometimes I understand God a little better from my experiences as a father. When my birthday or Christmas is approaching and my kids ask me what I want, I often reply that all I want is to spend the time together. It's not that all of the time we spend together is so great, I just like spending time with them, and I like it when they enjoy me. Sometimes they thank me for being their dad, and sometimes they thank me for the way that they were raised. Their gratitude makes all the difference. When they thank me for the work I have put into raising them, and when they find my time and energy helpful, that is a great reward for me.

I like spending time with my family. I hope that we all find it enjoyable. Sometimes that doesn't happen, but it is my hope and a great enjoyment when we do.

And then I hear a very soft, low, rumbling voice speaking with laughter in His voice, telling me,"*Yes child, that is what I am talking about. Just come to me! Just enjoy me.*"

I don't love my kids because they are good. They are good kids, but sometimes they do things that disappoint me. It doesn't make me want to quit being their father, and I don't love them less. In fact, before my granddaughter was old enough to do anything good or bad, I loved her without any reason, other than the fact that she is my granddaughter.

My difficulty is that I have a hard time really believing that God loves me. I am simply not all that good. I know the thoughts that linger in my mind, the feelings that sometimes embarrass me, and the many ways that I fail. How could God love me when He certainly knows how bad I really am?

Then I remember what I want from my children.

Simply that they remember that I am their father and that they might find the time to enjoy me.

Before Jesus told his followers to "Go into all the world," [23] He told them to remember Him. He told them to "Do this in remembrance of Me." [24]

I have wondered what it might have been like to be with the disciples when they uncorked a bottle of wine with some unleavened bread to eat and drink. I wonder what their conversation was like as they remembered being with Jesus. I suspect one of them turned to Peter and said, "Remember when you walked on the water with Jesus, Pete?" And he might have said, "Yeah, but remember when you woke Him up when we thought we were going to die? Then Jesus simply told the wind to hush and asked us what we were thinking. Remember how we were so afraid? We really didn't understand did we?"

Can you hear them talking with new believers about the transfiguration and remembering the feeding of the five thousand and the feeding of the four thousand? How would they have told the story of the demon-possessed man in the tombs? How would they have told people about Lazarus coming out of the tomb wrapped in grave clothes?

I expect each story would end with them remembering how much Jesus loved them, and they would finish their wine and swallow the bread, knowing that He loved them enough that He was willing to give them His life.

I suspect they might steal a glance toward heaven, wondering if Jesus was on His way back for them. And then they would tell the new folks about the great love that Jesus has for them, and they would do their best to explain that what Jesus really wants is for them to turn to Him and enjoy Him.

I would like to have been a part of the conversation—to hear them remember and celebrate with them as they did. I would like to hear them explain that:

He simply wants us to come to Him.

He wants us to trust in His goodness.

He wants us to enjoy Him.

"Ask, and you will receive, that your joy may be made full." [25] —*Jesus*

I think that love and life are synonyms. There is no life without love, and there is no love without life.

I find it fascinating that humanity has been given the gift of creating new life through what we call "making love." Not all sex is making love, and not all pregnancies are a result of the love of two people—but love is the design. It is how life was meant to be recreated. Making love is part of His gift to us.

Life and love—I believe those who are looking so desperately for love, not the shallow syrupy commercial love that we're being sold in the market place but the bottomless, authentic, and excessive love that God offers us—those who are looking for that love are very close to finding the riches of life that we are desperately searching for. Our problem is that we fall so easily for lovers that promise us life but then turn on us and only suck the life from us. There is only one lover who can give us life and will not take life from us.

I picture myself standing with the twelve, next to Peter, after many of the followers had left Jesus, because what he told them was too hard to listen to. After watching them all leave, Jesus turned and asked the twelve if they wanted to leave too. Peter said, "Master, to whom would we go? You have the words of real life—eternal life." John 6:68(The Message)

Where would we go?

There is nowhere else. There is no one else. Jesus has the words and is the Word of life. In Him is life. It is often confusing, sometimes frustrating, sometimes disappointing that it isn't working out the way I want it to.

Yet in all of my confusion, He asks me to trust Him. The chaos is meant to drive us to Him. He really likes being with us, being a part of our day, being included in our parties and alongside us in our work.

He really likes us. After all, He made us. He just wants us to go to him instead of all the other places we go searching for life.

I wish I could offer you a reliable method or procedure to follow that would take you to Jesus but it would be like telling you how to fall in love. There are no prerequisites to be met and no rules to follow. We simply grow to like someone who already likes us.

How does one fall in love with God? How do you go to Jesus?

If I would have been standing with Peter and the twelve when Jesus asked the question and Peter replied that there is nowhere else to go, I expect I would have been as or more confused than they were at the time. Confused that Jesus, the one that had come to save them, the one they had been waiting for didn't fit into the expectations of what a savior and messiah would look like. But maybe in the confusion, I would have turned to Peter with a smile and a nod and said, "Jesus loves me this I know," and followed Him anyway.

Maybe.

If I speak with the eloquence of men and of angels, but have no love, I become no more that blaring brass or crashing cymbal. If I have the gift of foretelling the future and hold in my mind not only all human knowledge but the very secrets of God, and if I also have that absolute faith which can move mountains, but have no love, I amount to nothing at all. If I can dispose of all that I possess, yes, even if I give my own body to be burned, but have no love, I achieve precisely nothing.

This love of which I speak is slow to lose patience—it looks for a way of being constructive. It is not possessive: it is neither anxious to impress nor does it cherish inflated ideas of its own importance.

Love has good manners and does not pursue selfish advantage. It is not touchy. It does not keep account of evil or gloat over the wickedness of other people. On the contrary, it shares the joy of those who live by the truth.

Love knows no limit to its endurance, no end to its trust, no fading of its hope; it can outlast anything. Love never fails.

For if there are prophecies they will be fulfilled and done with, if there are "tongues" the need for them will disappear, if there is knowledge it will be swallowed up in truth. For our knowledge is always incomplete and our prophecy is always incomplete, and when the complete comes, that is the end of the incomplete.

When I was a little child I talked and felt and thought like a little child. Now that I am a man I have finished with childish things.

At present we are men looking at puzzling reflections in a mirror. The time will come when we shall see reality whole and face to face! At present all I know is a little fraction of the truth, but the time will come when I shall know it as fully as God has known me!

In this life we have three lasting qualities—faith, hope and love. But the greatest of them is love.

I Corinthians 13
The New Testament in Modern English, J.B. Phillips, Macmillan Publishing Co.

Footnotes

---

[1] John 7:37, Matthew 7:7,8, Revelation 22:17
[2] Luke 6:31
[3] Psalm 46:10
[4] Psalm 81:12, 13
[5] John 15:5
[6] Matthew 11:28
[7] Matthew 22:36-39 The New International Version
[8] Matthew 16:24
[9] Romans 8:28 The New King James Version
[10] John 8:11
[11] John 14:6
[12] John 10:30
[13] John 14:16,23
[14] Hebrews 13:5
[15] John 21:15-17
[16] Mark 14:29
[17] Mark 14:66-71
[18] John 15:13
[19] Matthew 16:25 The New King James Version
[20] Matthew 13:45
[21] 2 Samuel 12:1-7
[22] John 2:1-10
[23] Mark 16:15
[24] 1 Corinthians 11:24
[25] John 16:24

You can read about the author at www.earthbornllc.com or email Steve at steve@earthbornllc.com.